Down To Earth Psychology ...

"This book has the rare quality in the area of psychology of being simple, easy to read and very informative. I feel it's a must for adolescents and young people studying marriage and/or family living."

Don E. Shaw, Coordinator of Health Education, Jefferson County Schools, Colorado

"In Walking on Air, readers learn to appreciate where they are coming from, to feel better about themselves and learn not to take life too seriously. Each chapter contains two or three points that can be used in a practical way."

Maggie Rennert, Book Reviewer, KCFR Public Radio, Denver, Colorado

"Walking on Air Without Stumbling is a layman's self-help book on re-examining ourselves and how we deal with our not-so-simple but almost—to-happen problems... free-flowing, easy style that emphasizes simple, concise readability."

Irma Wyhs, *Lakewood Sentinel,* Lakewood, Colorado

"I couldn't put your exciting book down until I'd finished it. Then, I was sorry I couldn't 'do it all over again'...I gave it a quick overlook, and I finally just gave in and read the whole thing cover to cover non-stop."

Virginia Johnson, retired civilian Air force employee, Denver, Colorado

Walking on Air Without Stumbling

Walking on Air
Without Stumbling

H. John Lyke, Ph.D.

Jeanne Peterson

Norma —
Thanks so much for all your
help and enthusiasm for all
of my writing endeavors. You
are a true patriot in every
sense of the word. With deep
appreciation and love —
H. John Lyke
11/19/12

Authors Choice Press
New York Lincoln Shanghai

WALKING ON AIR WITHOUT STUMBLING

Authors Choice Press
an imprint of iUniverse, Inc.

iUniverse books may be ordered through booksellers or by contacting:

iUniverse
2021 Pine Lake Road, Suite 100
Lincoln, NE 68512
www.iuniverse.com
1-800-Authors (1-800-288-4677)

Because of the dynamic nature of the Internet, any Web addresses
or links contained in this book may have changed
since publication and may no longer be valid.

The information, ideas, and suggestions in this book are not intended as a substitute for professional advice.
Before following any suggestions contained in this book, you should consult your personal physician
or mental health professional. Neither the author nor the publisher shall be liable or responsible
for any loss or damage allegedly arising as a consequence of your use or application
of any information or suggestions in this book.

Illustrations by Will LeVett

Second Edition

Originally published by Ripon Community Printers

ISBN: 978-0-595-47421-9

Printed in the United States of America

Dedication

For my mother, father and my two brothers, Doug and Ned, who so willingly and lovingly supported all of my creative endeavors, regardless of how 'far out' they might have seemed at the time, and for Richard R. Waite, friend, colleague and clinical psychologist <u>par excellence</u>, who has taught me much about the human condition.

H. John Lyke

For Harney, who has put up with my various imperfections with loving patience and reasonably constructive criticism for so many years.

Jeanne Peterson

TABLE OF CONTENTS

In This Ring . . .

In This Ring . . .
(Something About the Authors)

John Lyke, Ph.D., has had a private practice in psychology for some sixteen years. He is also a professor, a student counselor, and a consultant at a home for disturbed children. He plays jazz drums, is an avid jogger, and has been happily married to the same woman for 26 years. Also, for the past few years, he has spent some of his spare time inventing a game called "Gone Bananas."

He did this because he has always felt that it is important to be able to laugh at the human condition, to be aware of the times when you are taking yourself too seriously. He also has discovered that when you spend most of your waking hours either working with disturbed and troubled people or teaching classes in abnormal psychology, you tend to lose your own perspective. Working on the game was therapeutic for him; it is based on *normal* psychological motivations — getting psychic rewards for playing the stock market, going to college, receiving psychotherapy, or just having fun at a party.

His family was very helpful; some of them made suggestions for the board or chance cards, and all of them exhibited remarkable patience with what must at times have seemed an unreasonable obsession on John's part. It was important to him to have the game internally consistent, based on real psychological principles, making allowances for the different temperaments of players — and of course, above all — fun to play. *(For more about the game see page 289).*

Jeanne Peterson has a B.A. in chemistry from Carleton College, but spent only a brief time working for money before settling down to marry, take care of three children, and do a little volunteer work: writing publications for the League of Women Voters, writing fund-raising shows for her church, writing press releases for various good causes. She and her husband have been married for 33 years.

Well, John's game was finished, except that he had eleven pages of rules, which even his staunchest admirers found a bit daunting. Jeanne agreed to work on the rules, and by the time they had been revised a few times, the two authors (hereinafter referred to as "we") had agreed to collaborate on a book about psychology. The theory, as you might expect, is John's; the writing is Jeanne's.

We chose a circus theme for the cartoons, because — well, life is a bit like a three-ring circus, isn't it? From the point of view of the audience, you have to keep your eye on what you presume to be the main event. From the point of view of the performer, unlike those in a real circus, we all tend to go through life sadly underrehearsed; we are all on a tightrope, not quite sure whether Fate plans to catch us deftly this time or whether, if we miss, we are working with a safety net. That's the human condition.

The book has taken longer than we thought it would, but we have enjoyed working together on it, and we hope you will enjoy reading it. The chapters are short and reasonably self-contained, so that you can start on page 1 and go on from there, or you can dip into Freud or Mental Disorders or Marriage, or whatever interests you at the moment.

2

There is a pertinent question which you may be asking yourself (we certainly asked ourselves): Is the world really crying out for yet another popular psychology book? What is there that hasn't already been said by thirty or forty authors of other popular psychology books?

Well, we find ourselves in profound disagreement with the current trend in psychology self-help books. We don't believe that you necessarily become a mature, well-adjusted, creative person by being your own best friend, looking out for number one, or getting rid of your erroneous zones by ignoring the needs of everybody else and providing your own self-esteem.

We don't believe that basing your life on one or another of the current simplistic formulas is going to be very productive for you in the long run. We do believe it may be very destructive to those around you in the short run.

You won't find a simple formula in this book. We hope you will find some entertainment and some useful information. The human psyche is a complex structure with a built-in tendency to get itself maladjusted. The more you know about how it works, the more likely you are to save yourself — or maybe your friends and relatives — needless psychological pain.

We don't have any guaranteed answers (we don't believe anybody does, really). We do have some suggestions that John has found useful in his professional life. Maybe one or more of them will be helpful to you, or to somebody you know.

We're all caught in the same human predicament: we all put off doing things we should be working on, we hurt others intentionally or inadvertently, we have trouble expressing our real feelings, we make wrong choices.

Why?

If you can get in closer touch with the various forces in your head, if you can recognize what your own needs and the needs of those near and dear to you are at the moment, you can have more control over your own psychological processes, and therefore over your life.

"The unexamined life is not worth living." That is as true now as it was when it was first written.

This book is intended to help you examine your life, and by so doing to make that life more satisfying.

It's also intended to be fun to read. We hope you like it!

Changing Times

Changing Times
(A Brief Glance at History)

No wonder so many people are neurotic. No wonder our mental hospitals are overcrowded. No wonder we suffer from stress diseases. Surely no other generation of human beings has had to cope with such rapid change in technology and social expectations. If you are reading this book, you are probably old enough to have lived through two American "police actions," Korea and Vietnam. You may remember World War II, or the Great Depression, the stock market crash, perhaps even World War I. And now we have the energy crisis, turmoil in the MidEast, stagflation, schools which turn out illiterate graduates, women demanding equal rights, other women demanding protection of traditional family values, men claiming reverse discrimination, government interference in every aspect of our lives. Human beings were not designed to take this degree of stress, right?

Wrong. If you take even a cursory look at history, you will find that most people, certainly most people in the western world, have always lived in changing times. They have always had to cope with stress, and some periods have been far more stressful than our own.

It goes without saying that war and revolution provide abrupt changes and major stresses for their participants. What about the peaceful periods? When you look back in time, it's tempting to round off the corners, so to speak; to characterize an era by its outstanding leaders or its major political events, or perhaps by its effect on later periods. Living through a given period of time feels different to different groups.

Take Jane Austen who died in 1817, and was writing in the late 1700's and early 1800's. The upper middle class provincial people about whom she wrote seem stable, unworried, concerned about petty matters of precedence, etiquette, and above all, money. In the larger world, the Napoleonic Wars were in progress, and the American and French revolutions had already taken place.

Far more important to more people, the Industrial Revolution was in full swing. Power tools meant more efficiency, but they also meant factories. Cottage industry could not compete with centralized workplaces; people left the country to find jobs in the new industrial cities. Power tools needed coal for energy, and thus began the practice of sending children (who worked cheaper than grown men) into the mines. While Jane's people chatted about dowries and preferments, hundreds of thousands of working people suffered violent dislocations of their way of life. Stressful indeed, but most of them survived, and some of them even prospered.

Or look at the Victorian era: a long, prosperous, mostly peaceful reign. But during this period the steam locomotive was radically altering the concept of "a day's journey from home." No longer was the horse and carriage the measure of distance, or the wagon a measure of freight loads. The telegraph and the telephone made instant communication a reality; the photograph preserved sights and the phonograph preserved sounds.

And Darwin, Marx and Freud were writing books which would shock the Victorians as much as Brahe and Galileo had shocked their own contemporaries by suggesting that perhaps the earth was not, after all, the center of the universe. Having someone else challenge your deepest beliefs — "What do you mean, the sun doesn't go around the earth?" "Of course man was a special creation!" produces a lot of anxiety.

Now all of this is rather recent history; these people were essentially moderns, with modern problems and rapidly changing technology.

The Romans, some two thousand years ago, were also rather modern people. In spite of their odd-looking clothes, they lived, in many ways, pretty much as we do. They had banks, insurance, cheap souvenirs, factory-produced pottery, dry cleaners, and mortgages on their real estate. They even had the equivalent of a car rental service — you could pick up a horse and chariot at the gate of one city, change it for a fresh one at the gate of the next city, and so proceed across a good part of Europe. You could vacation in Egypt (many a fine old Roman name is scratched on one pyramid or another) and you could do it on a letter of credit, so you didn't have to carry much cash with you.

The Romans had our annoying combination of rising prices and rising unemployment, and the Roman government tried to cope by printing more money. Under the Empire, the silver denarius was no longer solid silver — it turned into a sandwich coin, like our Susan B. Anthony dollar or the last Kennedy halves, with a thin coating of silver on each side and cheaper metal in the middle.

If it's any comfort to you, the Romans also had to cope with religiously inspired uprisings in the Middle East and in Ireland.

But that sort of thing was for the provincial governor and the professional soldiers to deal with;

meanwhile, the middle class Romans back home had indoor plumbing as well as the famous Roman baths; their kitchens had double boilers, colanders, and commercially bottled seasonings. They had glass in their windows and pictures on their walls, and they complained about taxes and the deterioration of the public schools and the loafers on welfare just as we do.

The farmers knew about fertilizers and crop rotation and insecticides and contour plowing. They wrote books on how to get the hens to lay more eggs, better ways to cure hams, and how to dilute honey that had gone bad with new honey to get a product that you could sell to the city slickers who didn't know any better.

Now this is a book on psychology, not on history, but sometimes it is easier to understand ourselves after we have gained a little broader perspective on humanity in general.

Each of us is a unique human being. Collectively, however, we do not form a unique generation. People through the ages have been worrying and (fortunately for us) writing about similar concerns, and have come to remarkably similar conclusions. It's time for us to rethink some of them.

The generation gap

Here is part of a letter: "I sent my son to town to sell some produce, and I told him to come back the same day with the money. But he ran into one of those so-called philosophy teachers — and now he outdoes his teacher in the horrible things he's copied from him. It makes me shudder to look at him: his hair is long and he won't comb it, he goes about half naked, he doesn't wear shoes, he doesn't wash, he doesn't work. He doesn't pay any attention to the farm or to his mother and me; he says he doesn't owe us anything, he hates farming and is scornful of money. He has no reverence for anything; he says everything is just a combination of atoms."

Now, this kid is clearly one of those for whom the "No Shoes, No Shirt, No Service" signs were designed. He lived near Athens about 2300 years ago.

When you stop to think about it, isn't it surprising that we are still here and still human? Almost everyone who has ever held forth on the subject has concluded that the younger generation is lazier, more disrespectful, and less intelligent than the older one; and think how long we have been going along on our downhill path!

Juvenal, a Roman satirist, wrote around 50 A.D.: "Do you teach public speaking? What iron nerve you need while your class, by the score, knocks off tyrannical monarchs. Each schoolboy, in turn, gets up, and standing, delivers what he's just read sitting down, in the most monotonous singsong. This is the kind of rehash that kills unfortunate teachers. It's always the fault of the teacher if his students aren't thrilled to the core of their moronic beings when they bore us to death with the villain from Carthage. Name what amount you please — I'd be perfectly willing to pay it if the boys' fathers would hear their orations as often as I do. It isn't easy to keep your eye on all the students, keeping them under your thumb, seeing to it that they don't play dirty tricks on each other, or develop some of the nastier habits. According to their parents, that's your job — and your pay, at the end of a year, equals a jockey's fee if he's ridden only one winner."

Why is it that down through recorded history, most people have looked on the old days, the days when they themselves were children or very young adults, as the *good* old days? If their children get driven to school, they themselves walked or took a bus; if their children walk a mile to school, they walked four or five (more often than not in a blinding blizzard, while wearing hand-me-down boots with holes in them). The Egyptians, the Greeks, the Romans — all had a generation gap.

In an evolving society, there is always tension between generations. The younger generation's new ideas and new values produce change — for better or for worse. At first glance, the older generation is usually inclined to see the change as a lowering of standards, a dangerous radicalism, an indefensible apathy — whatever it is, it's not good.

This is only natural: we all tend to feel that our own beliefs are the right beliefs, and that the world would be vastly improved if everybody agreed with us. We all tend to resist change; change is painful. And when our own children question our values — well, of course there is a generation gap. With good will on both sides, we can bridge it.

Woman's place

All the cultures with which we are most familiar have been, or still are, run by men. Woman's place, therefore, is what the men of a given place and time want it to be.

The Bible furnishes some good examples: although the time frame extends over some thousands of years, the culture is Hebraic and heavily patriarchal. The vision of the ideal woman, however, changes from book to book.

The king of Persia renounced his former queen and replaced her with Esther because his advisors pointed out that if Queen Vashti got away with turning down a last-minute invitation to the king's banquet, every man in the kingdom was going to have trouble convincing his woman that he was the master of the household and was to be obeyed without question.

There are Biblical women who shyly do their father's or their brother's bidding, and others who take things into their own hands, even to the extent of killing the enemies of their country. Thanks to St. Paul's misogyny, the whole tone of the New Testament, except when Jesus himself is speaking, is distinctly anti-feminist.

On the other hand, that unnamed woman in the last chapter of Proverbs, the one whose price was above rubies, not only got up in time to fix breakfast for everybody, saw to it that her family was admirably clothed, and wove enough linen that she had some to sell — she also ran a sideline in handmade belts, and in her spare time dabbled in real estate. Her husband, meanwhile, sat at the city gates and accepted congratulations from the other men whose wives were not quite so hyperactive.

To turn Freud's question, "What does woman want?" around — what do men want women to be? The answer seems to be, "Somebody who will admire, respect, and obey me because I am a man."

At some times and in some places, women are thought of as the practical ones, the ones who can run a big household — but are incapable of abstract reasoning. Sometimes they are thought of as the frail ones, the ones who must be protected from the harsher realities of life (if bearing fifteen or twenty children is not considered one of the harsher realities of life). At all times, in the literature written by men, they are "the other;" man is the standard, and woman is the strange, almost-human creature who is not a man.

Here's a Greek (4th century B.C.) on the subject: He had been recently married; his bride was not yet fifteen, and had been admirably brought up to see as little, and hear as little, and ask as few questions as possible. "I had to give her time to grow used to me," he says, "but when we had reached a point where we could talk easily together, I told her that she had great responsibilities: she would have to keep stock of everything brought into the house; oversee all the work that went on; superintend the spinning, the weaving, the making of clothes; train the new servants, nurse the sick. Of course, she would stay indoors. I myself like to start the day with a long ride in the country, but naturally that was out of the question for her. However, I told her, she could get plenty of exercise, at the loom, or making beds, or supervising the maids. Kneading bread is said to be as good exercise as one can find. All that sort of thing would improve her figure and her complexion — very important in keeping herself attractive to me. And ever since, my wife has done just as I taught her."

And here's a Roman (1st century A.D.): This is a bit of friendly advice to an acquaintance who is about to be married. "Surely you used to be sane, Postumus, are you taking a wife? Can you be under her thumb, while ropes are so cheap and so many? When there are windows wide open and high enough to jump down from, while the Aemilian bridge is practically in your back yard?" Women, he points out, are notoriously unfaithful, extravagant, cruel, deceitful, overeducated, and unwilling to have children. But even if you can find the rare exception — "Let her be well-behaved, good-looking, wealthy, and fertile; let her have ancestors' busts and portraits over her hallways; let her be more intact than all the pre-ravished Sabines;

let her be a rare bird, the rarest on earth — who could endure to live with a wife endowed with every perfection?"

Woman's place in the modern world is still somewhat doubtful. In 1979, Pope John Paul II responded to Sister Theresa Kane's request that nuns be considered for all ministries within the church by suggesting that she should stop wearing modern clothes and go back to the traditional nun's habit. Four Orthodox rabbis have succeeded in restricting the circumstances under which Israeli women may have abortions. The United States Congress has prohibited using Medicaid funds for abortions except when the life of the woman is endangered. A handful of male state legislators in various states are succeeding in withholding the final ratification of the Equal Rights Amendment. Meanwhile, the President is recommending that women as well as men register for the draft.

Woman's place, in other words, is changing right now — but it still seems to be based heavily on responsibilities, while her rights depend on the whims of men.

Changing jobs

Technology is changing so rapidly nowadays that schools are pointing out, rather defensively, that they are trying to train students to handle jobs that don't exist yet; what a good teacher tries to do is get the kids to be flexible, because only God knows what's going to happen in the next decade or two, let alone the next generation or two.

When sewing machines were invented, what did the seamstresses do? When typewriters were invented, what did the clerks (who had spent years perfecting their copperplate handwriting) do? What did the buggy whip manufacturers do, or the men who delivered milk in horse-drawn wagons, or the icemen, or the lamplighters, when technology caught up with them? They did what we all must do; they adjusted to changing times.

As a matter of fact, some of the most enormous future shocks must have happened in prehistoric times. Pretend you are a hunter in a hunting-gathering society some 30,000 years ago. You and your male buddies are responsible for chasing down the occasional mastodon, driving it into a pit, and hacking it up. It's exciting, it's dangerous, and you and the other hunters are much admired by the rest of the tribe. Actually, however, most of your calories come from the fruits, nuts, berries, and grain that the women and children bring in. (This is the way it works in hunting-gathering societies today, and it's probably the way it worked in prehistoric times; meat is an occasional treat, not a staple).

And one day your mate says to you, "Honey, I have a surprise for you. I have tamed a pair of goats, and now the nanny goat is going to have a kid. Have you ever thought how convenient it would be to raise animals intead of hunting them? We could use the milk, and the wool, and the meat, and we wouldn't have to keep packing up the family and following the mastodon herds. Yes, of course I know goats aren't as big as mastodons, and it would take a lot of them to get the meat you could get out of one mastodon, but just think — they would be *right there* when you want them."

And before you know it, you have stopped being a mighty (if somewhat inefficient) hunter and are now a rancher. That sort of thing can be hard on a man.

Government interference
The infernal IRS is breathing down our necks, the

EPA is telling us what we can't do with our own land, the FTC is protecting or overprotecting us from false advertising, the FBI is tapping our phones and making lists of our friends and acquaintances, and the local school board is insisting that our kids have all their shots before they will begin teaching them sex education, humanism, and all sorts of other undesirable things. Has any government in history meddled in the private affairs of its citizens to this extent?

Well, Peter the Great went around cutting off the beards of his boyars; Frederick the Great insisted that the old women who sold vegetables from street stalls should keep knitting when they weren't waiting on customers; Charlemagne began a great tradition of religious intolerance when he insisted that all the pagans he conquered had to become Christians instantly. In Robin Hood's day, you will remember, all the forests and all the game in the forests belonged to the king, and hunting without a license got you killed. Rome set hours during which nobody but the Vestal Virgins could ride in a chariot within the city limits; Athens gathered juries by dragging people in off the streets. Government has always interfered in the lives of the citizens; it's just that in various other times the interference tended to be more personal and somewhat more eccentric. Now it's more even-handed, perhaps, and certainly more bureaucratic, but it's probably no more pervasive than it used to be.

Health care

Our health care, whether you are considering mental or physical health, is far from perfect.

Mental patients are being released to their communities (with the help of a large battery of recently developed drugs) rather than being kept in large

17

custodial hospitals. Surely this is a good thing? It is if the patient really has a community. Unfortunately, many of them have been confined so long that they have lost touch with family and friends; they don't know how to cope with ordinary affairs such as shopping and getting from one place to another; and too many of them wind up in the locked wards of nursing homes which have no mental health specialists.

This is a difficult problem for our society, and so far our solutions are less than ideal. However, if you look back into history — we're not doing too badly compared to some of our ancestors. The Bible is full of people "possessed by devils." They tended to get run out of town, if not stoned to death. During the Middle Ages, they got burned or drowned as witches. Shortly after that, a more enlightened age built asylums — places of refuge — for them. The most famous is probably St. Mary of Bethlehem in London — otherwise known as Bedlam. Patients were kept chained to the walls, bedded down on straw, underfed, and whipped at regular intervals to encourage them to return to their senses. Fashionable people regularly enjoyed spending an hour or two poking and prodding them with sticks to see what they would do.

We aren't perfect when it comes to the care of the physically ill, either. Oh, we can save lives that would have been lost a few years ago. Fewer mothers and babies die, if the mother has been under a doctor's care during pregnancy. There are remarkable new prosthetic devices to help those who have lost an arm or a leg. Drugs are much more sophisticated than they used to be; physicians are much better educated than they used to be.

The only trouble is that all this new sophistication in

medicine has made the cost escalate so much that one catastrophic illness can wipe out the life savings of a reasonably well-insured middle class family. There are people who stay home and die because they decide they can't afford to be hospitalized.

This is not good. But on the other hand — would you like to have been a leper (or have had some skin disease that could have been mistaken for leprosy) in the days when you had to ring a bell to announce your approach, and when you had to beg for a living? Or would you like to have had smallpox, pneumonia, or even a broken leg, when the universal first thought of any physician was to bleed the patient, no matter what was wrong? Or would you like to have exerienced one of the great plagues which swept over Europe and wiped out (in three passes) half the population?

World War II was the very first war in history in which more soldiers died of combat wounds than of secondary infections, epidemics of typhoid or dysentery, or malnutrition. Our health care isn't great — but it's better than it used to be.

Coping with our own changing times

Life in the immediate future is not going to be easy for most of us. We are going to have to cope with an energy crisis, inflation, unemployment, and maybe even war.

Life never has been easy; it never will be.

We need to keep a sense of perspective. If you were not alive here and now, where would you prefer to be? Who would you prefer to be? And when?

Victorian England? (OK if you are male and middle or upper class; otherwise, forget it.) Ancient Greece? (OK if you are between wars, not a slave, not a woman.) The Middle Ages? (Even the Popes had problems with politics and had to have large standing armies.)

Ancient Egypt? (Who do you think built all those pyramids?) A native American before the white invasion? (The skeletons at Mesa Verde indicate that most of them died young, with severe arthritis, teeth which had been ground down by chewing on corn mixed with the inadvertent stone powder which came from grinding it, and often with tuberculosis as well).

Since we are living in the here and now, we may as well make the best of it. This is not to say that we should sit back in resignation or complacency; far from it. Each of us has a responsibility to improve our own contemporary world — our own little corner of changing times. It won't be easy, but what that is worth doing ever is easy?

Who Says I Don't Know What's
Going On in My Own Head?

Who Says I Don't Know What's Going On in My Own Head?
(SIGMUND FREUD)

You may not care much for what you know about Freud. Indeed, anybody who could look around at Viennese social organization in the late nineteenth century and then say, "Woman! My God! What does she want?" was singularly lacking in perception, empathy, and several other qualities which one might wish one's therapist to have, right?

Nevertheless, Freud was a creative genius and the founder of modern personality theory. Although parts of his theory of personality development have been discarded by a number of therapists, and although some (notably radical behaviorists) reject the whole thing, we believe that his concepts of *psychic energy*, of the *unconscious forces in the mind*, and of the *critical stages of personality development* are not only valid but very useful ideas.

Psychic Energy

Suppose you have just finished climbing Pike's Peak (nimbly avoiding the cable cars and the automobiles); it has been a long, exhausting climb. Now here you are at the top, feeling very pleased with yourself, and enjoying a magnificent view. But you're also tired and hungry. Before you start down, you eat a candy bar or some raisins, and you sit down and rest awhile. Everybody knows that you have a limited amount of *physical* energy, and that it must be restored at frequent intervals by food and rest, especially if you've been doing something in the way of strenuous physical exercise.

Psychic energy works in somewhat the same way: you have a finite amount of psychic energy at any given time, and it, too, needs to be replenished at intervals.

For example, let's suppose you've just come home from a particularly grueling day at work. Your supervisor was even more obnoxious than usual, your accounts didn't balance, and you had to wait twenty minutes on a windy corner for the rest of your car pool to turn up.

Your spouse, meanwhile, has also had a frustrating day, different in detail but equally ghastly.

This is not the time for the two of you to work on the income tax (unless you look on that as a recreational activity) or decide whether Junior really needs braces on his teeth. You'll be much better off if you take a walk, read a book, watch TV, take a nap, have a snack, a cup of tea. Psychic energy can be replenished by food or rest, or by doing something — something undemanding — which you enjoy.

Psychic energy is depleted by any mental or emotional activity; it doesn't need to be as unpleasant as the example we gave above. You may have had a very enjoyable, stimulating day, but mental or emotional stimulation of any kind — good or bad — draws on your psychic energy, and you need to do something to build it up again.

How does your mind work?

In mysterious ways, most of the time. What you are aware of thinking is only a very small part of what's going on inside. The unconscious forces in your mind are constantly playing tug of war with each other, and what you do depends on the relative strength of one force or another at any given time.

Your *conscious* mind is the surface part — you are aware, for instance, that you are reading this book. If somebody should ask you what you had for dinner last night, or whether you liked the movie you saw a few days ago, you could probably come up with an answer without much thought. That's your *preconscious* mind — all the things which are, so to speak, sitting there on the top shelf ready to be lifted out if you need them; you're not aware of them at the moment, but they are fairly easy to bring into awareness.

Down in the bottom of your mental cupboard is your *unconscious* mind: all the stuff you've been tucking away over a lifetime. It's pretty cluttered and rather grubby, and you have a hard time finding anything at that level. However, things keep fermenting away down there, and influencing your conscious thoughts and feelings.

If you can't reach your unconscious, how do you know it's there?

Dreams, slips of the tongue or pen, hypnosis, and free association techniques all seem to indicate the existence of the unconscious.

Take dreams:

John sometimes uses hypnosis to help clients get in touch with their unconscious. He suggested to one client that she should relax into a light hypnotic state, and try to get in touch with her unconscious mind. She reported when she awoke that she had dreamed — she was sliding down a long playground slide, and at the bottom was a pile of muck — in other words, she had slid toward her unconscious mind, and realized that there was a lot of stuff down there which was pretty messy.

When we decided to write this book, Jeanne had a very detailed, vivid dream. She was sitting on the patio with a number of friends and relatives, watching the elderly family cat, who had suddenly abandoned his usual dignity and was frisking like a kitten, leaping into the air, tangling himself up in a ball of string, and finally jumping into the swimming pool, where he promptly sank. Nobody else on the patio noticed what had happened. Jeanne rushed over, fished out the cat, and said, "Well, that's good; she's going to be all right."

She woke up with that sentence echoing in her mind, and wondered why she had spoken of a male cat as "she." An instant later she knew why: the cat was Jeanne herself. She had been wondering whether adding this writing project to her other responsibilities was foolish — kittenish. Her conscious mind was telling her that it was not going to be too much of an entanglement; she could fish herself out all right.

When John was in therapy, on his way to becoming a psychologist, he was working through some things related to separating himself psychologically from his parents. John had been telling the therapist about his father's prowess in fishing — one year he had caught the second largest North American trout for the year, and the next year he had gone back to the same area, and come up with the first prize trout.

The night before John's next therapy session, he dreamed that two trout were on a stringer and had their heads out of the water, gasping, obviously about to expire. John didn't know what the dream symbolized, but the therapist suggested that the two trout were John's parents, and that John was in the process of killing his dependence on them. Once the interpretation had been made, John had that "Yes, of course that's what it meant!" feeling you sometimes get about dreams: he got some insight into how important his parents were in his life, and how central they were to his thinking.

This may be an even better example: one of John's colleagues recently had a vasectomy. Now, this was not something forced upon him: he and his wife had agreed it made sense, the psychologist didn't have any lingering *conscious* thoughts about wanting more children; he knew that the operation would not affect his masculinity.

His unconscious apparently thought otherwise. The night before the operation, he dreamed that all his fingers were much shorter than they had been. And the night after the operation, he dreamed that he was out in a field with a long-barreled shotgun, potting rabbits — except that the rabbits kept merrily hopping around and thumbing their noses at him; he wasn't hitting any of them.

Now this symbolism is about as Freudian as you can get (fingers and guns both being common phallic symbols). Does this mean that Freud was right in his interpretation of dream symbols? Not necessarily; what it does mean is that this psychologist's professional training was based on Freudian theories, and so when his unconscious wants to tell him something, it chooses Freudian symbols to get the message across.

If you dream about guns, fingers, trains, church steeples — are you using masculine symbols? Or if you dream about rounded hills, tunnels, corridors — are you using feminine symbols? Maybe and maybe not. It depends on your own private associations with these things. Freud himself once said, "Sometimes a cigar is only a cigar."

You can usually tell whether a dream has

significance by the way you feel in the dream or just after you wake up: if you feel a lot of emotion, if your dream *feels* as though it's trying to tell you something, it probably is. Pay attention!

As for slips of the tongue or pen, have you ever found yourself saying cheerfully to a friend who has stayed too long, "Well, I've certainly enjoyed your visit; don't hurry back!" Or closed a letter to that cousin you never much liked by writing, "With out best wishes," when you meant to write "With our best wishes?"

Free association, another indication that something is going on at levels which are ordinarily out of your reach, can be a help in therapy. If you spend an hour in a relaxed position saying whatever comes into your head, you are getting into closer touch with your unconscious, and providing your therapist with useful clues as to what is troubling you.

John has a word association game which he uses in class. Each student writes a paragraph on his or her most traumatic experience. John collects the papers and chooses three or four of the most dramatic ones, sends their authors out of the room, and reads the papers to the rest of the class. They pick out emotionally loaded words — "plane," for example, if one of the papers describes a terrifying parachute jump; "fire" if there is a paragraph about a devastating blaze.

The authors are now called back, and told to try to keep the class from guessing correctly who wrote which paper. But the class can tell — every time — by noting the reactions of each person to the key words. It's simply impossible not to show some reaction to a word that carries a big emotional load for you, no matter how hard you are consciously trying to avoid it. Your unconscious won't let you get away with it.

The forces in your mind

In Freudian terms, these forces are the Id, the Ego, and the Superego. They are not, of course, specific parts of your brain like the cortex or the cerebellum. Think of them as poetic concepts or analogies, or as facets of your personality.

The Id (Latin for *it*) is the "I want" part of your unconscious. It operates on the pleasure principle — it is interested *only* in seeking pleasure and avoiding pain. It has no sense of time — everything, for the Id, is in the present. The Id wants what it wants *right now;* it is not aware of the passage of time. This means that it doesn't care to save for a rainy day or to eat the ice cream *after* the vegetables. It also means that if something worked once for you, no matter how long ago, your Id is going to encourage you to keep right on using that same ploy, even though it may not be a bit appropriate for your present circumstances.

For example: perhaps when you were in kindergarten, you didn't like riding the school bus. And perhaps if you dawdled around long enough, your mother would get the car out and drive you to school herself.

Well, your Id doesn't know that you're now 35, and that when you put off paying those bills or getting rid of that trash or writing that report, you're going to wind up in bankruptcy court, or in trouble with the board of health, or out of a job, as the case may be. Anyway, nobody (probably including your mother) is going to give you a free ride. Your Id doesn't know that, but *you* do — don't you?

Which brings us to the Ego (Latin for *I*).

A baby, psychologically speaking, is all Id. The Id is the source of all psychic energy, and as personality develops, part of its energy is used to form the Ego.

This is the "What's Best" part of you — the part that is, we trust, in touch with reality; the part that decides to cut down a little on the martinis and save for next year's vacation (you would have to fight your Id on this), to get out of teaching and into the supermarket business, or vice versa; to get married or divorced or have a child or not have one — all for more or less rational reasons.

The Ego is partly conscious and partly unconscious; a lot of our decisions are strongly influenced by things going on in our heads of which we are not aware. It operates on the reality principle — it is capable of postponing immediate gratification in favor of a long-range goal. Not that the Ego always decides on postponement, of course. Any time you decide anything at all, whether or not it's a sensible decision, that's your Ego functioning. The Id acts on impulse; the Ego makes decisions.

The Superego (*Above-I*) is the "I Should" part of your mind. It is your conscience, if you like to think about it that way, except that it operates at an unconscious as well as a conscious level. Depending upon how you were brought up, it may be chatting to you about going to church, giving up smoking, eating an apple a day, keeping a kosher kitchen, or never leaving your hands so idle that the devil will find work for them to do.

Now you may, over the years, have *consciously* changed your mind about some of these precepts (most of which were built into you before you were five or six years old) but your Superego may still be making you feel guilty about them.

Your Superego may be right, of course; maybe you're simply getting overly self-indulgent as the years go by. (If you've been reading many of the popular psychology books, you probably are!)

On the other hand, it may be wrong; your Superego tends not to want you to have any fun at all.

If it is too well developed, you may have trouble making up your mind about anything at all, because your Superego keeps saying, "Well you *should* — but on the other hand, maybe you should also —".

If everything is going along all right, if you have what is known in the psych. business as a "well-integrated personality," you'll feel pretty good most of the time, you'll be reasonably efficient and happy, and you won't be aware (except perhaps when you're dreaming) that all these forces are down in there slugging it out with each other.

All three forces are necessary to your personality. Don't think of the Id, for instance, as "bad" because it is, by normal standards, selfish or self-centered, interested only in looking for pleasure and avoiding pain. The Id is the basic, rock-bottom basis of personality, the source of the other facets, and therefore absolutely necessary. It keeps trying to express itself, and if things go well, it keeps getting squashed — but only partially squashed — by the Superego. All this creates a healthy tension.

You didn't think tension was healthy? Well, if you didn't have some, you would be in the position of a piece of flotsam (or worse yet, jetsam), at the mercy of the wind and waves.

So much, for the time being, for unconscious forces in a healthy balance. If things are not going along so smoothly — well, we'll get to that later, in the chapter on "Mental Disorders."

Now we come to a more controversial topic — critical stages of personality development. We believe that critical stages exist, all right; John's version appears in another chapter. However, we think the Freudian version is somewhat unconvincing. For one thing, he assumed that personality was set in the first few years of life, and that all neurotic problems which appeared later had their basis in something that happened in those first few years.

For another thing, Freud's delineation of critical stages seems to apply much more closely to men than to women, to people of his era rather than ours, to Western society rather than to the world in general. It probably fits Freud himself best of all — he used to spend the last half hour of each day analyzing himself, and checking the validity of his ideas by seeing how well they fit his own feelings and inhibitions.

Be that as it may, Freud was a pioneer in the field of critical stages, as in so many other areas of psychology. His lineup — simplified perhaps to the point of oversimplification — goes like this:

First comes the *oral stage*. A new baby (which, you will remember, is all Id — all pleasure-seeking) gets all its satisfaction through its mouth. The sucking sensation is pleasant in itself, and the baby soon learns that it leads to a full tummy, too. For maybe the first six months of life, the baby's life is centered around its mouth as the place to take in comfort. When the baby begins to acquire some teeth, the mouth has a double significance — it's still the place to take in nourishment and to feel pleasant sensations, but now it also becomes a means of expressing other feelings. The baby can and does still suck, but now it can also spit out food it doesn't like, and it can bite things — or people — to let the rest of the world know how it feels about its life.

Next we have the *anal stage*. The baby, you understand, has been weaned by this time. And has hated each minute of the weaning process. Mother, in

32

this respect, may know what's best, but the child tends not to be convinced of it. Life for an infant, after all, is full of unpleasant surprises: first you are thrust out of a warm, cozy, soft womb into a big noisy bright world where you have to keep breathing, where you aren't automatically fed through an umbilical cord but have to suck to get any nourishment. Now you are being weaned — removed from a soft, cuddly breast full of delicious milk and being asked to believe that strained spinach from a hard spoon is an adequate substitute.

But worse is yet to come: your mother has decided that you are old enough to begin potty training. You are no longer the center of your universe — she seems to feel that she ought to have some say as to when and where you empty your bladder and your bowels. (Not behind the couch, let us say).

Well, this is, according to Freud (and according to common sense, as a matter of fact) both a good thing and a bad thing. You and your mother are struggling for control. She is bigger and brighter than you are at your present stage of development, so she's going to win, and this is going to be tough on your Id. On the other hand, this very struggle is what is helping you to realize that you are one person and she is another; that you are one thing and the world at large is something separate from you.

Next we get into the *phallic stage.* This is where a child develops a sense of self-worth, mainly by competing with other people, begins testing reality, learning how to cope with more and more kinds of problems. Freud calls it the phallic stage because children are very much aware of their genitals at this period (about three years to five years old is where we are) and do a lot of studying of comparative anatomy. (This is probably more true of little boys than little girls, but practically all kids of this age like to play doctor).

Was Oedipus a nervous Rex?

Now we come to the Oedipal complex. (Jeanne, incidentally, does not believe a word of this).

This is more or less the gospel according to Freud: The little boy is in competition with his father, and wants to possess (in any sense you care to read it) his mother. However, his father is considerably bigger, stronger, and tougher than he is, and he is afraid that if he lets his father know how he really feels (which is roughly, "Why don't you drop dead and let me marry Mama?") his father will castrate him. Therefore, he decides that the best he can do is to imitate his father, be as much like him as possible, and instead of marrying his mother, settle for sitting on her lap now and then or trying to please her by running errands and washing his hands before dinner.

John's son, during the time when if Freud was right he was being swayed by these forces, liked to play cowboy, and John was being very cooperative, "dying" when the boy shot him with magnificent drama. Judy, meanwhile, was fixing supper, and much as John urged him, "Hey, why don't you shoot her?" Chris absolutely refused; killing Daddy was one thing, killing Mama was something else again. Freud would certainly know what to think of that. On the other hand, the kid may just have been a realist: if you kill Mama while she's fixing your dinner, you're going to get pretty hungry.

If you are a girl, it's even tougher. You identify with your mother at first, since she is usually the most important parent for any infant. Then as time goes on, you move over to admiring your father, wanting to sleep with him, wishing your mother were dead — and

34

then you have to move back, somehow, toward identifying with your mother. The girl compares herself with father, brother, or some other male figure, and realizes that she doesn't have a penis. Then she checks Mama, and realizes that she doesn't have one either. For some reason, she leaps to the conclusion that Mama has castrated her, and that if she tells Mama how she really feels about her, even worse things may befall — who knows, maybe Mama will follow through by cutting off her head.

So she decides that the only way that she can be whole again is to have a baby (preferably a boy, of course) by her father. With a little bit of luck, she will, by the time she gets old enough really to manage this, have transferred her feelings from her father to a suitable boyfriend. Meanwhile, she identifies with her mother.

No wonder Freud felt women were a little strange!

Jeanne's feeling about this is that penis envy (taken as a literal thing) is pure myth. What little girls really envy is the freedom of little boys to play outside while the little girls are helping with the dishes or keeping an eye on the baby. If childhood training gets more unisex, the whole thing may well disappear. We'll see.

Now, you may go through all these stages and resolve your problematical Oedipal complex satisfactorily, but still have some very serious psychological problems later on. John and Jeanne agree that Freud was right about a lot of things, but sometimes for the wrong reasons.

Back to childhood psychological development: After you have worked through your Oedipal stage, you go into a period of latency, when nothing much happens psychologically speaking, until you're in your early teens, at which point you enter the genital stage —

when everything you haven't worked through at the appropriate point as an infant will rise up and give you fits. However, you do have a second chance to work through some of these stages as you are going through adolescence.

If you muff it that time, too — you will arrive at adulthood with a bunch of unmet needs that you aren't even conscious of having, and you will be neurotic and need a shrink to help you unravel your past and get those needs finally, if somewhat belatedly, met.

Or so, at least, says Freud.

How's Your Balance?

How's Your Balance?
(Mental Disorders)

Are you crazy?

Statistically speaking, the answer to that is — probably not, but you may well be a little flaky.

Flakiness, of course, is a matter of degree. While relatively few of us spend much time, or even any time, in a mental hospital, practically all of us have periods of life, or certain areas lifelong, or both, in which we're not operating on all cylinders. It's something like driving an eight cylinder automobile with three badly fouled plugs. The car does move, after a fashion; it may take us where we want to go, but not as quickly, economically, smoothly or pleasantly as it should.

You can think of mental health as forming a continuum — with perfect mental health, which probably nobody has, as the ideal at one end, and serious mental illness at the other.

Or you can think of it as a tightrope — that's you balancing in midair, with various stresses and strains pulling at you. When you consider what a complicated affair life is, it's really not surprising that many people lose their balance now and then.

How normal are you?

Are you unhappy for no particular reason? Do you have a poor sense of self-worth? A sense of incompleteness? Limited creativity? (Never mind if you think you have no talent; everybody is potentially creative, and if you aren't, either you have not yet found your particular milieu, or you are neurotic).

Before we get any further into neuroses, we should point out that the American Psychiatric Association has just agreed to take the word 'neurosis' off its list and replace it with the word 'disorders'. This is because that august body (like us) realizes that mental health is on a continuum, and its members have decided that dividing mental difficulties into neuroses and psychoses serves no useful purpose. We disagree. Meanwhile, if you prefer to think of yourself or your friends as disordered rather than neurotic, please feel free to do so.

Do you have difficulty in making decisions? Do you find yourself going back over past decisions — time and time again — wondering if you were wrong? Then you have some degree of neurosis, and psychotherapy may help you understand your problems and take control of your own life again.

People whose mental health is pretty good feel happy most of the time, they don't have too much pain or anxiety, they feel in control of their lives. They are productive at school or work, and they have friends. They fit in with the *reasonable* expectations of society.

Fitting in with the reasonable expectations of society does not mean that you have to be a complete conformist. Parts of our society are sick, and should be changed; the movers and shakers of society do not fit in, and this is all to the good.

But if you get your kicks out of hurting other people, it doesn't matter how happy you are — your mental health leaves something to be desired. The same thing follows if your actions are so peculiar that *most people* look on you as strange. Very likely, in that case, you *are* strange, and everybody, including you, would be better off if you got some professional help.

Are you neurotic?

In the chapter on Freud we mentioned the forces in your mind: the Id "I Want"; the Ego "I Choose" and the Superego "I Should." Now if you have a major conflict among these three forces, with your Id, for instance, wanting a bright red Mercedes and your Superego chanting, "Use it up, wear it out, make it do, or do without," while your Ego is standing around baffled, you have a *neurosis*.

A neurosis can take many different forms, some of which are pretty dramatic. In the case above, for instance, you might have a conversion reaction, converting your mental confusion into physical symptoms. You could perhaps go blind or become paralyzed, so that you can't drive a car, in which case your Superego could convince your Id that now you don't really need a bright red Mercedes.

A hundred years ago, conversion reactions were rather common. They are much rarer now, perhaps because medicine has advanced somewhat; it's easier to tell when symptoms are caused by your mind and when they are a sign of something physically wrong. One example is the Case of the Paralyzed Hand. It is perfectly possible, of course, to have a hand paralyzed due to injury or disease; in this case, the lack of feeling and lack of ability to move the hand follow nerve patterns. In the case of a hand paralyzed due to a conversion reaction, however, the symptoms follow a "glove" pattern, as though the afflicted person were wearing a glove that kept the hand from feeling or reacting. This is not the way the nerves are arranged, however, and therefore the hand can be cured with mental rather than physical treatment.

Another dramatic (but extremely rare) form of

41

neurosis is dissociated personality, as in *Sybil* or *The Three Faces of Eve*. In cases like this, the personality fragments itself, and each fragment takes turns controlling the body. Some of the fragments know each other — that is, they remember what their common body was doing while under control of one of the other fragments — and some have no recollection of what happened while they were unconscious, or not in control. "Eve," for example, became pregnant in one of her manifestations, and awoke under control of another part of her personality with no recollection at all of previous visits to the obstetrician.

Think of the advantages of this sort of neurosis — you can be sexy, greedy, childlike, or whatever — but who can blame you? It's not really *you* — it's a separate part of your personality which you can't control. More important, even you don't have to blame yourself — your Id is having a field day, and your Superego, for the time being, is just not operating.

There are advantages, all right, but the price in fright is horrendous. "Eve" never knew when she might awaken as somebody else, bewildered, uncertain as to where she was or how she got there, afraid that she had done something dreadful while under control of — well, of what? If you can't trust your own mind, what can you trust? If you can't stay in control of yourself, you're in a panic-making situation.

It's this sort of thing, no doubt, that made people believe in witchcraft. There are still a lot of common phrases which reflect the old belief in demonic possession: What came over you? I must have been out of my mind! He was absolutely beside himself! I wasn't myself.

Of course, you don't have to have a dissociated personality type of neurosis to get some of this effect;

it's just a very dramatic example.

Anybody who drinks a little too much now and then is likely to provide a milder example of a free-wheeling Id.

John now and then plays drums in a Dixieland band. He was doing this one evening when he noticed an acquaintance making a determined pass at a pretty girl. All very well, except that the man's wife was also among those present, and the girl was the wife's best friend.

The man (at his wife's insistence) came to see John professionally a few days later. His defense was, "I'd had too much to drink; I wasn't myself."

Actually, of course, he was right in a way — he wasn't his usual self, with his Id, his Ego, and his Superego in their normal balance. His Id had, for the moment, taken over, while his Superego was hampered by his alcoholic intake. However, his Id must have had a yen for his wife's friend, or maybe for any pretty girl; if he'd been sober, he just wouldn't have *acted* on that impulse — or perhaps even consciously realized that the impulse was there.

In this particular case, the man came to see John a few times and then terminated therapy; his discussions with John were beginning to get him in closer touch with his unconscious, and he didn't like what he saw. He wanted, in other words, to keep the lid on his Id.

Neuroses of more common kinds

Dissociated personality is very rare indeed; a neurosis is more likely to manifest itself in less vivid, but sometimes equally crippling ways.

One of the disconcerting things about a neurosis is that you are in touch with reality — that is, you *know* you're being irrational, you know you're irritating the people who love you (or used to love you — how long can they continue to like anybody as silly as you are?) — so you think you should be able to grit your teeth and tell yourself you're not being sensible, and just go ahead and get well. In most cases, all of this self-knowledge and all of this determination doesn't do you one bit of good; your symptoms are still right there.

A neurosis can take a lot of different forms, and can range from mildly distracting to severely disabling. One of the most common kinds — about half of all neurotics suffer from it — is an anxiety neurosis.

The sky is falling

How do you recognize an anxiety neurosis? The key word is *free-floating* anxiety. You're tense and anxious a lot of the time, but you can't really pin down what it is you're afraid of, or if you do try to pin it down, it's a little unconvincing.

For instance, you might find yourself worrying that your ten-year-old will be run over by a car on his way to school. You live on a quiet street, the school is only two blocks away, your child is a responsible type who not only knows he should look both ways before crossing a street, but actually does it. Nevertheless, you worry yourself into a fit every time he leaves for school, and every time he's five minutes late getting home. You're really afraid of something else, and part of you knows it.

You may not latch on to anything this specific. You may just wake up from a sound sleep and find yourself shaking with terror, your heart pounding away at twice its usual rate. A few experiences like that, and you're afraid to go to sleep in the first place.

You may be doing some perfectly normal, un-frightening thing — shopping, cooking, typing — and

44

suddenly find yourself paralyzed with fear, for no good reason. And the fact that you know there's nothing to be frightened of is the most frightening thing of all.

You find yourself in a vicious circle: the physical symptoms of fear — the cold sweat, the speeded up heart, the dizziness — are terrifying. They have happened once, so they may happen again. You're afraid they might happen again. This makes you more anxious, more tense, so that more likely than not, they *will* happen again, and then you're even more frightened. The whole thing is very discouraging indeed.

What kind of people get an anxiety neurosis?

Freud felt that any kind of neurosis in an adult meant that he or she had an unresolved Oedipal conflict. John does not agree; he thinks that people who have an anxiety neurosis have a poor sense of self-worth, and are afraid of competition.

Now a poor sense of self-worth does not mean a lack of competence; some people who seem to the rest of the world not only competent but extraordinarily creative and successful have a poor sense of selfworth. They go through life feeling, "Well, I've been successful so far, but *I* know it's just because I've been lucky, because I've been able so far to deceive everybody about what a clod I really am; and my luck can't hold forever. One of these days I'm really going to flub it, and then everybody will know what I already know — that I really am not the hotshot they all think I am!"

Now, if you keep thinking like that, of course you're going to go around feeling anxious. You must keep in mind through all this that the victim of a neurosis does not go around *consciously* telling himself all this — this is happening at an unconscious level.

45

Take heart, though; while this isn't something that most people can work through all by themselves, it is something that a good psychotherapist can help you work through. In the example we used a couple of pages ago — you are afraid your child is going to get run over on his way to school — maybe if you didn't have that child, and that house in the suburbs, you would be back in school yourself becoming a paleontologist; much as you consciously love him, perhaps there's a part of your unconscious that feels you'd be better off without him; since you can't admit that, you develop an irrational fear that something bad is going to happen to him. Or maybe it's something else entirely. A therapist can help you find out.

Phobias

In a phobia, you're pinning your anxiety to a specific thing.

Sometimes a phobia is an overreaction to something that a lot of people are somewhat afraid of — snakes, perhaps. The difference is that a phobia is an *irrational* fear — you are afraid of garter snakes as well as rattlesnakes, and even snakes safely behind glass in a zoo make you shudder.

Or you're afraid of heights, not only when you are standing at the edge of a cliff, but when you're looking out of an observation tower, or even going up in an elevator.

There's an enormous list of phobias; some of the common things people are afraid of are: acrophobia (high places); agoraphobia (open places); claustrophobia (closed places) — which just about takes care of places, doesn't it? Others are: monophobia (being alone); ocholophobia (crowds); zoophobia (animals or some particular animal). If you know a little Greek, you can make up your own.

Jeanne, for instance, when she is wandering around working up to writing something, feels she is suffering from ergaphobia (fear of work).

Where do phobias come from? Sometimes from a frightening experience — if, as a child, you are bitten by a dog, you may need a lot of convincing before you stop being afraid of all dogs. Sometimes by being associated with a frightening experience — if you get hit on the head by a stray golf ball just as you are about to pick a handsome specimen of amanita muscaria, you may find that the next time you see an amanita muscaria, or maybe even any kind of wild mushroom, you feel nervous. (If you plan to *eat* an amanita, you should feel nervous!)

Sometimes a phobia is a coverup for something else. Suppose you have been slogging along doing an adequate job in the production department on the ground floor. Then you get a promotion — great! But you are pretty sure that the promotion puts you well over your head in responsibility — you really can't handle the new job, and pretty soon the company will find that out and they will fire you. The new job is on the fifteenth floor. Now if you develop a phobia that won't let you work on the fifteenth floor (acrophobia) or ride in an elevator (claustrophobia) you can get a lot of sympathy — and your old first-floor job.

Phobias can succumb to behavior modification — you begin by thinking about the thing that frightens you, and instead of shying off when you get anxious, you keep on picturing the scary situation: the dog sees you coming along the sidewalk, he growls, you keep on coming closer, he lunges at you, you try unsuccessfully to fend him off, he bites you, you crawl to the nearest hospital and begin a series of rabies shots — all this, of course, in the safety of the therapist's office. After a

47

number of sessions like this (sometimes surprisingly few) you discover that you are no longer afraid of dogs — "walking through" your worst fears in a safe situation has taken away your phobia.

If your therapist is any good, he or she is also finding out at the same time why you have the phobia in the first place, so that whatever your underlying problem is, it won't pop out in the form of other flaky behavior.

Children sometimes develop a phobia about going to school, and this "walk through" approach has been very successful in curing that.

First, of course, you should do a little investigating: your child may have a perfectly sensible reason for hating or fearing school — an unfair teacher, a bullying classmate, a problem with hearing or vision, subject matter which is too hard or boringly easy, dyslexia — any number of things can really be wrong with the school or your child, and in most cases you can do something about it. But if it seems to be a real — irrational — phobia, you can find out as specifically as possible what your child is afraid of, and then get him or her to pretend to be walking to school, seeing the building getting closer and closer, feeling sick, wanting to turn back, going on — well, you get the idea. The reality just isn't as bad as the fantasy.

Any abnormal psychology textbook is capable of going on for several hundred pages about various neurotic problems and what to do about them; we have chosen these either because they are so bizarre or because they are so common. We're about to get to the most common problem of all.

Depression

One out of eight Americans suffers from depression. When you consider what life is like, that figure seems pretty low — sooner or later, everybody suffers some sort of loss. It may be the death of a friend, separation from a husband or wife, a severe setback in your career, leading to loss of self-esteem, a refusal from the girl (or boy) of your choice — you name it, life will provide it.

When you suffer a heavy loss of some sort, you react with sadness, maybe with anger — 'Why did this happen to me? What did I do wrong?' You may have trouble sleeping, you may lose interest in eating, you may get headaches. It doesn't seem worth the trouble to get up in the morning. Even getting dressed may stop being a routine, practically automatic process. You find yourself standing with a shirt in one hand and a tie in the other, making heavy weather of deciding whether they go together.

That's depression — but you can think of it as *normal* depression. After you work through your grief, decide how you are going to remake your life in your new circumstances, finish your mourning period, your depression will go away, usually gradually, sometimes rather suddenly. In the words of the old song, "The sun's gonna shine in my back door some day."

That's one cause of depression.

Everybody has mood swings — some days you feel particularly happy, energetic, with it — for no particular reason. Other days you feel moody, vaguely unhappy, dissatisfied with life — also for no particular reason. Those downswings are also normal. Only if they go on and on, or drop you really into the depths, are they abnormal.

Abnormal depression can range from mild to severe. Even a mild form is not something you have fun with.

Jeanne suffered from a mild depression a few years back. She's still not sure about the causes: a close friend had died of cancer about six months earlier, and she still missed him and thought about him a great deal; and she had been taking oral contraceptives for some years (one of the possible side-effects of oral contraceptives is depression).

Anyway, one night at a party she was listening to a string quartet and found herself sitting in a dark corner of the patio, weeping hopelessly at the thought that she was never going to become a concert violinist. Since she had never had any musical training — or particularly wanted to have any — this seemed peculiar, to say the least.

Things after that got worse: she cried a lot, often at most inopportune times, but the prevailing feeling was not so much sadness as a sort of gray hopelessness. Nothing was any fun any more, things she had always enjoyed doing were utterly boring, she didn't want to talk to most of her friends, she had to make a tremendous effort to get up in the morning, much less fix breakfast for her husband, wash dishes, see that the kids got off to school, take part in committee meetings — everything was hard, and nothing was interesting, and what was worse, life was going to be just that way forever. When you're really inside a depression, you can dimly remember that you used to get excited about politics, applaud a jazz band, enjoy gourmet cooking, love your family and your friends — but it doesn't *feel* real. Jeanne felt as though there were a glass wall (sorry for the cliche, but that's what it was like) between her and everybody else. She felt vaguely sorry for her husband and children, who were sympathetic and getting more and more worried — but she couldn't *feel* any warm emotions toward them. You got a promotion! How nice. You're having trouble with geometry? Too bad. You want me to go out to dinner with you? No, thanks. Jeanne kept plodding along, going through the motions; many of her friends, who had problems of their own, still don't know that she went through this.

After several months of this glooming around, she decided that the only logical thing to do was to commit suicide — life as it was was nothing to hang onto. She sat down one day and made a list of pros and cons — and the only con she could think of was that if she killed herself she would upset her family. All right, then the way to go was in an apparent accident. But how? It was winter, and climbing a mountain and falling off a cliff is a seasonal form of accident. Clean a gun? Nobody in the family had ever handled, much less owned, a gun (except when Harney was in the Air Corps). How about a car? She didn't have a car of her own and walking in front of some stranger's car seemed needlessly unkind to the stranger.

For some reason, at this point Jeanne's sense of humor came back; sitting around thinking of ways to do herself in seemed more ridiculous than harrowing. She stopped taking the Pill, and a month later felt fine. As we said at the beginning, she still doesn't know whether her depression was set off by the death of her friend, by the contraceptive, by both, by neither; or whether stopping the pill and shortly feeling better was cause and effect or coincidence.

Okay, that's a *mild* depression; she didn't have any physical symptoms except fatigue.

Clinical, physical symptoms of depression are: fatigue, insomnia, loss of interest in food, constipation, weight loss, headaches. (They could also be symptoms of something wrong with your digestive tract. See your doctor before you diagnose yourself as depressed).

We'll get into clinical symptoms further in the next chapter. Meanwhile, remember that when you suffer a real loss — separation from someone you love, serious physical injury or illness, loss of a job or office which meant a lot to you — of course you're going to be upset. Of course you need a time to mourn, to readjust. Of course you're going to feel depressed.

Being unhappy for a fairly short time (weeks or months, perhaps a year) is not a sign that something is wrong with you. As a matter of fact, if you didn't react that way it would be a much worse sign — inappropriate emotional responses (smiling cheerfully as you learn you have been clobbered in the election in which you have invested all your savings and a year of your life) are signals of very serious mental disorders.

But after you've had a chance to grieve, if you keep on being depressed, if you keep futilely wishing your life were the way it used to be, if you can't pick up the pieces and somehow redesign your life to fit your new circumstances — that's when you need help.

Have You Gone Bananas?

Have You Gone Bananas?
(Mental Illness)

The term 'mental illness' was first used some decades ago for two reasons. In the first place, 'crazy' or 'lunatic' were not very kindly terms; people tended to look down on other people who were labeled that way. 'Mental illness' sounded better; you can't help being sick, can you, whether it's from a physical or a mental cause? Unfortunately, society's judgment seems to be — you bet you can! If anybody has ever said to you, "You're sick!" or "That's really gross — that's downright *sick!*" you will appreciate that you haven't received a compliment.

The second reason for using the term 'mental illness' is that people working in the mental field learned that one form of mental illness — general paresis, the gruesome final stage of untreated syphilis — was caused by a specific microorganism. This raised hopes that perhaps all mental illness was caused by germs, or at least had an organic cause.

Nothing much came of this. Some kinds of depression seem to be caused by a chemical imbalance; others don't seem to be. Some kinds of psychosis can be controlled by drugs; others can't — although that's not to say that as yet undiscovered drugs won't be effective. Schizophrenia and depression seem to have a partly genetic, partly environmental, cause. That is, you may be predisposed to depression or to schizophrenia, and whether or not you ever develop symptoms will depend on how your life goes. If you never have to meet a heavy crisis at a time when your psychic reserves are low, you'll be O.K. Otherwise — you run more risk than the average person of crumbling — at least temporarily — under the strain.

Right now, most kinds of mental illness are still more or less mysterious. Why the term, then?

For one thing, it makes the therapist feel better (and perhaps the patient, and the patient's family). If you can give something a name, you have a feeling that you know something about it, that you may be closer to being able to control it.

For another thing, if you can classify symptoms, you ought to be able to find a therapy that works for one case and then extend it to other, similar cases.

At the present time (in spite of the fact that medicine is probably still more an art than a science) this works a lot better for physical disorders than for mental ones.

If a patient turns up with a high fever, a rash, and a positive streptococcus culture, you not only know what you're dealing with; you know what to do about it.

If a young patient becomes gradually more withdrawn and lethargic, it may be depression — or simple schizophrenia. While both are treatable, the youngster with depression, once through the crisis, has a high probability of leading a normal life; the one with simple schizophrenia is likely to get worse and worse.

If you have a friend or relative who seems to be acting strangely, try to get help — but be a little skeptical of the diagnosis. Jeanne has a friend who fell madly in love his freshman year in college. When the girl broke off their relationship, he found himself unable to study, unable to understand what was going on in class, unable to make even the simplest decisions. The diagnosis was simple schizophrenia, and the doctor who made the diagnosis predicted that he would have to be hospitalized for the rest of his life.

His family disagreed. He dropped out of school for a year, drifted around playing piano in places whose owners were about as peculiar as he was at the time, went back to college, finished a five-year course in physics and engineering and is now designing computers. He still has problems — don't we all? — and in the past eighteen years has had to be hospitalized twice for severe depression, a week each time. However, two weeks in eighteen years is quite different from a lifetime sentence to a mental hospital.

How do you know if you're really in trouble?

If you hear voices that nobody else hears, if you see visions that nobody else sees, there are three possibilities. You may have an extraordinarily well developed sense of hearing or sight. You may be a saint. Unfortunately, the most likely possibility is that you're a psychotic.

Psychosis is a loss of contact with reality under stress: a conflict between your Ego (I Choose) and the outside world. Sometimes it's a selective loss. That is, a psychotic under certain conditions can act perfectly normally, for the time being. In case of a fire in the hospital, for instance, psychotics have been known not only to save themselves, but to help the staff save other people. When the danger is over, they go back to being crazy.

This loss of contact with reality usually comes in the form of delusions or hallucinations. A psychosis can be treated in a mental hospital, or sometimes on an out-patient basis.

Some psychoses, as we mentioned earlier, seem to be caused by a chemical imbalance. Results with drugs such as lithium carbonate have been good with manic-depressive (psychotic) people, but not for people with neurotic depression. In the last twenty years or so a lot of new drugs have turned up which make the prospects for some kinds of psychosis a lot brighter than they used to be.

However, you might keep in mind that a psychotic who improves enough to leave a hospital and to stay out while on medication is not necessarily back to what the average person thinks of as normal.

Functioning after a fashion, yes; normal, no.

One woman who had been hospitalized for a number of years was followed wherever she went by large, aggressive, menacing grizzly bears. She and her doctors were delighted when they discovered a drug which allowed her to leave the hospital and go back to her former life as a housewife.

Not that the bears went away. They stayed right with her — but as long as she remembered to take the right pills every day, they hibernated. She had to dust around them, or shove them out of the way to get at the ironing, but they stayed asleep. However, if she forgot to take her medication, the bears instantly woke up and growled at her.

Other psychotics are luckier; some of them will never get any symptoms again as long as they keep faithfully taking their medicine.

Now, we feel (perhaps unreasonably) that if you are reading this book, you are not psychotic. However, sometime during your life you are very likely indeed to run into somebody who is. While we don't want to tell you more than you want to know about mental illness, we do feel that everybody should know at least a little something about it.

Psychotics can be dangerous to themselves or to others; they can and do kill themselves, sometimes after wiping out a dozen innocent by-standers, an estranged spouse, or somebody who just stumbled against them while running for a bus.

The other side of this is that many psychotics can be returned to normalcy by some form of psychotherapy. The thing is to catch them in time — before they get so out of control that they are dangerous.

If all the people you know at the moment seem to have all their marbles, maybe you'll want to skip this chapter for the time being, and come back to it if you need to sometime later. Otherwise, read on!

Psychoses and intelligence

Mental illness and intelligence — or lack of it — don't have much correlation with each other. It is true that brain-damaged children may have more emotional problems than normal children — maybe because their world is so much harder to cope with than our normal world, maybe because they tend to be treated different-ly, and come to feel that they are so different that they are unlovable. Poor people may have more mental illness than rich people — maybe because their lives are so much more stressful. Are rich people more intelligent? Sometimes, sometimes not.

But in general, you can believe the following old story:

A motorist, late for an appointment, is driving by a mental hospital just at dusk, when he feels a tire go flat. He steers onto the shoulder, jacks up the car, gets the spare from the trunk, takes the old tire off, puts the spare in position — and stumbles, sending all four lug nuts tumbling into the storm drain beside him, irretrievably beyond his reach.

One of the hospital inmates, who has been in-terestedly watching this whole episode, says, "Why don't you take one of the lug nuts from each of your other three wheels and put them on this one? That would give you three on each wheel, which should be O.K. until you can get to a garage."

The motorist, overwhelmed by this ingenious solution, says, "Uh, tell me, isn't this place a mental hospital? And you *are* a patient? How come you were able to think of something like that?"

And the patient replies indignantly, "Well, gee, I may be crazy — but I'm not stupid!"

The particular kind of mental illness which people get is related in complicated ways to their age, sex, life circumstances, heredity, and previous personality. Schizophrenia is in general a disease of the young. Depression hits more women than men. Paranoid schizophrenics tend to have been suspicious, 'paranoid' people while they were sane. Involutional melancholia hits middle aged people, usually women.

Here are a few of the more common kinds:

Psychotic depression and manic-depressive syndrome

We talked about normal and neurotic depression in the chapter on 'Mental Disorders.' Psychotic depression involves the same kinds of feelings, but can be much more severe. A patient in a psychotic depression can be agitated — unable to sleep, unable even to sit down, despairingly recounting over and over again the terrible crimes (usually imaginary) that have led to this dreadful — but in the patient's mind justified — punishment. "I was never a good daughter, I didn't love my mother enough, when she wanted me to wash the dishes sometimes I would — oh, God, I've lost my mind, I've lost my mind, it was when I had my wisdom tooth pulled, my mind came out when they pulled the tooth and now I've lost it. Oh, help me to get my mind back, help me to find my mind! I lost it because I'm such a terrible sinner, I didn't listen to my mother, and now she's dead, she's dead because I'm so wicked. . ."

Or a patient with psychotic depression can be in a stupor, unable to respond at all, having to be fed through a tube.

Or somewhere in between. Mental activity is slowed down and distorted, decisions are impossible. Conversation has a dreamlike, unreal quality: "Did you ask why I'm in the hospital? . . . Well, because. . . maybe . . . I'm so sad . . . I never thought I'd . . . What? . . . Oh, it's Tuesday, I think, and I've been here. . . maybe a week . . . or two . . . I'm here because . . . well, my liver has turned to stone, and above that I'm all hollow, there's nothing there . . ."

A patient in the agitated stage can kill somebody else, and any depressed patient is likely to kill himself or herself — especially when the depression seems to be lifting, and family, friends, and therapist may be feeling most encouraged. A *really* depressed patient can't summon up enough energy to commit suicide; the dangerous time is when things get just enough better to make thoughts of suicide possible, but not enough better to make thoughts of suicide repellant. Never believe in the old cliche that "people who talk about suicide never do it."

They do, they do indeed.

While depression is an *affective* (feeling) disorder rather than a thought disorder, severe depression can lead to disorders in thinking, almost as if the patient has to justify the mood. Thus, women who have never had any children will talk about what bad mothers they were, men will describe crimes they couldn't possibly have committed. These people are suffering so intensely that the human instinct for justice forces them to invent a crime to fit the punishment.

The victim of a manic-depressive psychosis gets the highs as well as the lows. This is a mixed blessing, however, since a psychotic high is not necessarily a euphoric one; it's more likely to involve agitation and a tendency to violence.

In fact, a manic-depressive in the 'up' phase is your good old-fashioned maniac beloved by gothic novelists — complete with glaring eyes, an inclination to hit you over the head with a baseball bat or perhaps strangle you with his bare hands — and the strength to do it.

A hypomanic, on the other hand, is living at just a little more intense level than the average person. If you are considering running for public office, try to get a hypomanic to be your campaign manager; he will be bubbling over with energy, drive, enthusiasm and ingenious ideas.

People with psychotic depression or manic-depressive psychosis tend to have acute episodes of illness which last a few months, interspersed with months — or even as long as ten or twenty years — of normal moods. Those who respond well to lithium can go for the rest of their lives with no further acute episodes.

Incidentally, you might be interested in some figures on what we in the United States spend on research:

In 1974, research on cancer (which affects more than 1 million people each year) got $568 million. Heart disease (which affects 15 million a year) got $190 million. And research on depression (which affects 19 million people each year) got $6 million.

Schizophrenia

'Schizophrenia' is not a very good word; it means 'split mind,' which has very little to do with schizophrenic symptoms. Schizophrenia, like cancer, applies to a large group of diseases with varying symptoms. Taken all in all, schizophrenics account for about half of all the patients in mental hospitals. It is a disease of the young: three quarters of first admissions for schizophrenia are patients between the ages of fifteen and forty-five.

Unfortunately, schizophrenia has a tendency either to recur or to become chronic, although a combination of chemotheraphy and psychotherapy can prevent this. The chemotherapy (major tranquillizers) reduces symptoms, while the psychotherapy gives the patient a chance to examine his or her life goals and to figure out ways to reduce stress.

John has had at least two recovered schizophrenics as students. Both of them were among the brightest students in class, really in touch not only with reality but with their own unconscious minds. He doesn't anticipate that either of them will necessarily have further problems.

Paranoid schizophrenia is the most common form; about half of all schizophrenics are paranoid. They tend to be brighter than most schizophrenics, but also more suspicious and less able to handle interpersonal relationships.

A schizophrenic may have delusions about only one rather small area of life — John once had a patient who believed that inanimate objects have feelings. He was a drummer, and he had to give up his profession because he couldn't bring himelf to beat those drums anymore. "It isn't so bad for the cymbals," he said, "they're tough; but those poor drums!"

More often, a paranoid schizophrenic will have a well developed delusional system, believing that he is the center of a complicated plot devised by God, the devil, people from outer space, the Communists, the FBI or the CIA. (Come to think of it, even a schizophrenic may sometimes be right!)

Or he may *be* God, the devil, a person from outer space, or an undercover agent. In any case, it's almost impossible to break up a really good delusional system. One patient thought he was a ghost. "Listen," said the exasperated therapist, "do ghosts have to shave?" "Of course not," said the patient. "Well, come over here and look in the mirror; see the stubble on your chin? So you can't be a ghost, can you?" "Gosh," replied the patient, "I guess I was wrong. Ghosts *do* have to shave!"

Paranoid schizophrenics are hard to treat because they are suspicious of everybody, including, of course, therapists, and trusting your therapist is the first step in psychotherapy. They tend to minimize their own unconscious and maximize everybody else's, so that there may well be a kernel of truth to their perceptions of other people's attitudes toward them. Should you run into a paranoid schizophrenic, the best thing to do is carefully remain nonjudgmental; otherwise you are likely to be built right into the delusional system, and it is not healthy to be perceived by a schizophrenic as one of the bad guys.

Another form of schizophrenia is *hebephrenia*. The original Hebe was the daughter of Zeus and Hera; she was the goddess of youth and cupbearer to the gods. Judging from the disease which is named after her, she must have been a giddy little thing, probably pausing frequently between pantry and banquet hall to take a nip of the nectar she was supposed to be serving the rest of the company. Anyway, hebephrenics are very silly, childlike, and tend to giggle a lot.

Simple schizophrenia usually starts early, sometimes even before adolescence. The victims of this disease gradually lose interest in everything: school, sports, friends, family, jobs — everything. It isn't that they can't achieve any more; they just don't want to. They won't clean their rooms, or even themselves; they won't bother to answer questions; they want to spend more and more time all alone.

Now, if you have a kid who exhibits some of these symptoms, don't just assume it will go away; if it's really simple schizophrenia, it will just get worse and worse, and eventually the kid will be more or less a vegetable.

On the other hand, don't panic. First, you might consider whether there is a loss of interest in everything, or just a substitution of interests. Choosing parties over homework or girls over hockey may not be what you would prefer your child to be doing right now, but it is not a sign of schizophrenia. Next, you might think about drugs. If your youngster has a bureau drawer full of mixed pills, or usually smells as though he's just been helping to burn down a rope factory, you probably have found the answer. Another possibility is mononucleosis — kids with mono have been known to fall asleep in the middle of a sentence.

If you do suspect simple schizophrenia, get help right away; prompt treatment can prevent further deterioration. The sooner you start, the more you'll have to work with.

Why do people go crazy?

Sometimes it's a response to unbearable strain. Remember that what seems like a relatively mild problem to you may constitute unbearable strain to somebody else. Adolescents, in particular, are already going through a time of turmoil, and a fairly small thing may be enough to upset an already precarious balance.

Sometimes, oddly enough, it's the only sensible thing to do. Suppose, for instance, that you are a woman who lives in a slum. You have an eighth grade education (but you read at the third grade level). You also have five small children, and a husband who beats you up whenever he's had too much to drink. You work part time cleaning offices, but you worry that your husband will hurt the children or set fire to the house while you're gone. You *can't* support the family and your husband *won't* support the family.

One day the whole thing is just too much for you. You begin acting so erratically that your neighbors, or the police, can't help but notice. Somebody comes and puts the kids in foster homes, and puts you in the local mental hospital. It's not exactly a glamorous setting, but it's better than what you've been putting up with for the past ten years. You're getting three square meals a day, nobody is beating you up, and although you may miss your children, and realize that they miss you, at least for the time being they — and you — are more or less OK. Finally, somebody else — not you — is taking charge of things, doing the worrying, doing the planning. In other words, going crazy can be a sort of rest cure.

It can also, in a weird sort of way, be fun. Acting irresponsibly, doing what you want to do when you want to do it, forgetting about possible consequences, can be a really delightful experience.

To take a very mild example, have you ever decided to pass up cramming for an important final exam in favor of going to a movie? Fun, wasn't it — at least until the next morning — letting your Id take over? That's the kind of feeling some people get when they decide to go crazy; they can — maybe for the first time since they were about two years old — say and do just what they want to do just when they want to. They don't have to be polite, considerate, thoughtful, or aware of future obligations — after all, they're crazy.

While some kinds of mental illness can be fun — in a way — they can also be terrifying. If something is wrong with you physically, even something rather serious, you more or less know where you are. You get the bone set, have the operation, take the medicine; you have some idea of how long you're going to be feeling ill.

Mental illness is much more amorphous and therefore much more scary. But it's not usually hopeless.

You may have noticed that the phrase we used back there was 'decided to go crazy.' This is not to say that anybody simply sits down and says, "Well, next weekend, I think I'll really spin off out of control."

We do believe that some part of the mind has said just that, and that with help, the whole person — the integrated personality, if you will — can *take* control again.

And that is the antithesis of mental illness and the essence of mental health — *you* are in control of yourself.

The Con Man

The Con Man
(The Sociopathic Personality)

You meet this really charming young man in a singles bar. Or maybe he's sitting next to you at a concert or a hockey game. You're not so likely to run into him at church (unless he's the minister's son) or at a meeting of your local Mental Health Association; he's not much into good causes unless they pay.

Anyway, however you meet him, your friendship progresses rapidly. He's solicitous, witty, and clearly infatuated with you. By the time a couple of weeks have gone by, you've dropped all your other friends and are seeing only him. Why not? He makes you feel great about yourself — when you're with him, you know you're not only marvelous to look at, but delightful to be with. He appreciates facets of your personality and your appearance that your friends and family have never noticed, or anyway never mentioned so flatteringly.

That dimple in your cheek — why has nobody else ever commented on it? You find yourself practicing a lopsided smile in your mirror, to bring out the dimple. You buy a honey-colored dress to bring out the color of your eyes — the eyes that you've heard your mother describe as "Well, I don't know, sort of tan. I'd always hoped for a really dark-eyed child." You try a new hair style which will bring out your high cheekbones. You stop buying *Reader's Digest* and begin substituting *The New Yorker* — to bring out the sophisticated sense of humor which your new friend so much admires. "Bring out" — that's the secret of his charm. You're still you, of course, but now you're a more beautiful, witty, self-confident you: the you that your more obtuse friends have never appreciated, but that he has brought out. You have never felt so good about yourself.

As time goes by, you may find yourself disturbed by some aspects of his life style. He's intelligent and charming — so why can't he keep a job? As you begin to piece together various anecdotes, you realize that he rarely stayed in the same job for more than two or three months. His explanations are plausible, but it does seem unfair that one person should have so much bad luck, should encounter so many people who are jealous, or stupid, or malicious. It never seems to be his fault when he's fired. The boss was certainly unfair in that case of the missing petty cash; after all, there were plenty of other people who could have taken it. And then there was the time the company (another company, of course) objected to a collection agency calling him during working hours. And the business about the overdrawn check — of course he could have covered it, and would have, if they had given him enough notice. After awhile, it occurs to you that it isn't a matter of one overdrawn check: it's a whole series.

He isn't always fired. Often, he quits. Just a couple of weeks ago, he mentioned to you that his employer said he was the best salesman the store had ever had. Today he tells you that he's left; the job just wasn't challenging enough.

He not only changes jobs, he changes fields. He's often worked as a salesman. He's dabbled in politics. He spent a couple of months raising funds for a local charity. He raised a lot of money, too; he's very persuasive, and he had a lot of good ideas for running the campaign. The charity, it is true, was disturbed to discover that 90% of the funds had gone for overhead. But you realize that that wasn't your friend's fault; of course you have to dress well and drive a good car when you are calling on prospects; how else can you inspire confidence and get a really sizeable donation?

You worry about his driving. He has a collection of speeding tickets that he's never done anything about, and he still drives much too fast. He's not worried, however; he explains to you that his reflexes are good (which is true), so there's really no danger. And as for the tickets — the courts are so backlogged that it may be years before they get to him — meanwhile, something will turn up. They'll change the law. Or he'll move out of the state. Whoever heard of anybody being extradited for traffic tickets?

One memorable evening, you get home from work an hour early and find him in bed with your roommate. She bursts into tears, flings some clothes on, and departs to visit her sister. He explains to you that of course, she meant nothing at all to him, it was just an experiment, she kept coming on so strong that he really couldn't help it, certainly it was the first — and of course the last — time; he will never, ever be unfaithful again, he can't live without you, he can't understand how it all happened, but he knows that you — being the sensitive, perceptive, understanding person you are — will give him another chance.

Being human, you do.

A week later, you see him coming out of your ex-roommate's sister's apartment. It takes him a little longer to convince you this time that this will *really* be the last time — but you forgive him again. He is so plausible — and you want to be convinced. How can you lose him? How can you live without the new you he's called to life, the delightful, charming, larger-than-life you that you are when you're with him?

You have another week or two together. Then he tells you he's had a telegram from the West Coast. His dear old mother urgently needs an operation, and he urgently needs $500 to supplement Medicare. He doesn't like to ask you, but you know if he sells his stock now, with the market down . . . if you could just lend him the money for a few weeks, until the market rebounds, as it surely will . . .

You never hear from him again. Did you really think you would?

You are now sadder, wiser, and $500 poorer. You have just had an encounter with a sociopath. (But just think: you might have *married* him! Really, you've had a lucky escape.)

This particular scenario may never happen to you. But since there are probably some 5,000,000 sociopaths in the United States today — and their number is growing — if you know, say, a hundred and fifty people, the odds are pretty high that you know at least one or two sociopaths.

Getting back to our script — what about your roommate? How *could* she get involved with the man you loved? The same way you did. She too enjoyed being seduced, enjoyed the appreciation of her subtle, hitherto undiscovered assets, enjoyed his sense of humor, his sophistication, his way of making her feel good about herself. Just as you did. Just as everybody does. Even professionals in the mental health field often get conned by sociopaths. Their charm is almost irresistible.

What is a sociopath, anyway?

Remember, this too is a continuum. The murderers in

Truman Capote's *In Cold Blood* were an extreme case of sociopathic personalities — one end of the continuum. At the other end are — all the rest of us more or less normal people. Anytime you find yourself wanting to get something for nothing, to take advantage of a friend or a stranger, to treat people as though they were objects to be manipulated for your convenience, rather than subjects in their own right — stop and think. You're acting like a sociopath. If you're somewhere in that normal range on your continuum (and if you're reading this book, you are!) you don't make a habit of this kind of thing. For a real sociopath, manipulation is a way of life.

The real sociopath, in spite of his intelligence and his charm — both of which tend to be well above average — has a very shallow, primitive personality. It's as though his ego were full of holes, forming a sieve through which drip all the guilt and anxiety that make most of us pay attention to our superego, or conscience. The sociopath *has* no conscience. In the moral realm he is operating as if he were two or three years old. You have to explain to a two year old that other people and animals have feelings, that they're not like his teddy bear, who doesn't mind being dropped out of a third floor window or left out in the snow.

The sociopath never really takes this in: to him, other people are around simply to suit his convenience. He can't ever form a warm, lasting relationship with another person, because he can't really believe that other people are real in the way that he himself is real.

Since he has no conscience, he has no guilty feelings. He will say he's sorry, that he'll never do it again, that he can't forgive himself — but he doesn't mean a word of it. He's just being manipulative. Again, he's operating at the level of a small child. A very young child can't generalize, can't reason that if he's been told not to take a piece of cake without asking, this means that he shouldn't take a cookie without asking. He will say, when scolded, that he's sorry, but he won't really know what that phrase means: it's just something to say to get Mommy to smile at you again. It's that way with the sociopath, too — you say you're sorry in order to get what you want.

With his primitive, almost nonexistent superego, a sociopath doesn't get the satisfaction that most of us do out of knowing we're doing something well, or being appreciated by other people. He has to get his satisfactions in some other way, and the way he does it is by manipulating other people into giving him something that he wants, usually something tangible — money, power, sex (or if he's conning a prison therapist — freedom).

Since he acts out his feelings when he feels them, he doesn't have any anxiety. He can't really believe that there ever will be a rainy day or an end of the road for him. And if he did believe it, it wouldn't bother him. Sociopaths simply don't get anxious.

What can you do for somebody like that?

Try to stay out of his way.

Not that that's easy — there's that abundant charm, that plausibility, that ability to make you feel great about yourself — for a while.

Traditional therapy doesn't work. In the first place, a sociopath will never ask for help, because from his point of view he doesn't need any; we should all be so happy! It's his family and friends who need the help, because a sociopath's road through life is strewn with the wreckage of other people's lives.

In the second place, therapy for most people works because they form an attachment to the therapist, and

74

really care what the therapist thinks of them. They'll work to change their behavior in order to earn the approval of the therapist. The sociopath, on the other hand, doesn't give a damn for anybody's approval; it's not part of his reward system.

Punishment doesn't work very well either. A sociopath is usually bright enough to avoid a lot of the punishment that ought to be coming to him, and even when things eventually do catch up with him, it doesn't bother him much. A lot of the effect of punishment on normal people is worrying about it, feeling anxiety about it. The sociopath doesn't feel any anxiety; he is living in the present moment only, not a bit concerned about the future.

How does a sociopath get to be one?

It starts very early in life, and maybe it's partly congenital. A large proportion of sociopaths — but not all of them — have abnormal brain waves. On the other hand some people who don't show any sign of being sociopathic have the same abnormal brain wave pattern.

It may be due to bad parenting. A large proportion of sociopaths — but, again, not all of them — come from broken homes, especially from homes where there was a lot of friction between the parents, and a lot of inconsistent behavior toward the child, before the final break (Of course, a lot of normal people also come from homes like that).

There are two kinds of family situations which seem particularly likely to produce sociopathic children. The first is one in which the parents are so angry with each other or so upset with each other that the baby is more or less ignored, or alternately ignored and punished.

The second — which produces most middle class

sociopaths — is a family which lays great stress on appearances. A politician's family, for instance, may take great pains to present a united public front, while all sorts of passions are boiling away in private. A young child is likely to get the message that what you *do* doesn't matter, so long as the neighbors, the public, the press don't find out about it.

Since you probably don't want deliberately to loose a sociopath upon an unsuspecting world (and you most certainly don't want to live with one) what can you do?

You can be loving, consistent, and not too severe (not so severe, that is, that your child learns to escape punishment by lying or by manipulating you) and hope for the best. You can, especially if you are male, try hard not to act like a sociopath yourself; many sociopaths have sociopathic fathers.

You may have noticed that we've consistently said "he" when talking about sociopaths. Practically all of them are male — why, nobody really knows.

Maybe you'd better just hope that all your children are girls.

There is one bright spot in this whole thing: most sociopaths grow out of it by the time they are 35 or 40. Nobody really knows why; perhaps their drives are weaker by that time, and they don't have to be sociopathic to satisfy their wants. Unfortunately, a sociopath can cut quite a swathe before he becomes a burnt-out case.

Remember that continuum?

Back toward the beginning of this chapter, we said that sociopathy forms a continuum, and there's a little of the sociopath in all of us.

This is especially clear when it comes to buying and selling. A good salesman has to block out part of his

76

altruistic nature when he's talking a customer into buying an Oldsmobile this year instead of a Plymouth. On the other hand, if he's really good, and wants repeat buyers, he won't run this approach into the ground — there's a delicate balance between persuading someone to spend a little more than he had intended to spend, and really conning him.

Meanwhile, the customer is also being somewhat sociopathic — trying to con the dealer into throwing in some free accessories or an extra guarantee. If everything works out, both sides feel satisfied with the bargain: the customer has talked the salesman into some concessions, and the salesman has talked the customer into some options.

If things don't balance so neatly, one side or the other (and it's usually the customer) is going to feel cheated. When John was a poverty-stricken graduate student with a young wife and a new baby, he found himself signing a contract to buy a set of en-cyclopedias, and an atlas, and a set of children's books, and a handy index. As he watched the salesman drive away — in a Cadillac — he said to his wife, "You know what? We've been taken." So what did he do about it? Nothing. Why? First, because he didn't want to acknowledge that he had made a bad choice (this is called repression). Second, because he felt ashamed of having been manipulated, and this hurt. Third, it was just easier to forget the whole thing (except when the monthly payments came due).

So much for salesmen (and we hope you're reading carefully; we're not saying that salesmen are sociopaths!)

The charm which sociopaths seem to exert so effortlessly is a decided asset in a lot of fields — politics, the ministry, medicine, therapy — we're not against charm per se. The important thing here is the end in view. If you're trying to seduce somebody into doing what you want because you want it — and you don't care what happens to the other person — you're being sociopathic. If you're trying to seduce somebody into doing what you want because you believe it would be best for the other person — that's a different kettle of fish.

Just be sure you're not fooling yourself, as well as your partner, if you're taking the second course.

If you are of a philosophical turn of mind, you might think about Kant's categorical imperative, which can be loosely interpreted as, "If everybody in the world were doing what I'm doing, would the world be better or worse?"

On a more personal level, try to decide whether you're rationalizing, making up reasons that sound good but aren't your *real* reasons for trying to persuade another person to change.

The touchstone is probably this: what kind of relationship do you have? Do you empathize with the other person — do you understand where he or she is coming from? Is this a long-term relationship, one that you expect to continue? If you're involved in some sort of one-shot deal — say, trying to talk the lady at the car rental place into a reduction on the basis that you asked for a red car and all she has is a blue one — your motives are probably somewhat impure, and you're being a bit sociopathic. On the other hand, if you're trying to persuade your wife to stop smoking, your motives may be mixed (you don't like the smell of smoke; someday she's going to burn the house down; it's a filthy, expensive habit which is keeping you from spending as much as you'd like to on Scotch) — but you know and she knows that it would actually be for her own good to stop smoking. Assuming you plan to keep your wife awhile longer, you probably are not being sociopathic, you are being caring. (Not, of course, that persuasion does one bit of good in a case like this, until the smoker himself decides to quit — but you do at least have the satisfaction of knowing that you're not acting like a sociopath!)

Are sociopaths mentally ill? Not by the standard definitions. Psychotics are out of touch with reality; sociopaths are clearly in touch with reality (unless you define other people's feelings as "reality.") Neurotics feel guilt and anxiety; sociopaths feel neither. They simply have primitive, unfinished personalities, and maybe, therefore, the rest of us should feel sorry for them — but they certainly don't make it easy!

*How Do You Know
You're Soulmates?*

How Do You Know You're Soulmates?

(Choosing Partners)

A lot of the discussion in this chapter applies to any long-term relationship, whether heterosexual or homosexual, legal or informal, but we're going to relate it particularly to marriage, because marriage is still by far the most common intimate relationship in this country, and the one where the law always steps in when you want to end it.

People go into a marriage hoping, expecting, even being completely confident that it's going to last. Why are they so often wrong?

There is, of course, no simple answer, but we'll give you some of what we consider to be the major factors.

In the first place, most people get married for the wrong reasons. Most people will tell you they got married because they fell in love with each other. Now this is indeed a compelling motive, but it is in itself fraught with danger — because when you are 'in love' you are not seeing the object of your love at all clearly, but rather a sort of ideal projection — and it is also usually combined with one or more other reasons, sometimes conscious and sometimes not.

Social pressure

A few decades ago, social pressure played a big role in encouraging marriage — early marriage. You finished high school, maybe you went to college or even graduate school. You dated various people or you went steady with the same person from junior high on.

And then you got married.

If you weren't married by the time you were twenty-five or so (especially if you were female), your friends and relatives began looking at you oddly. Your mother began commenting wistfully about how adorable her friends' grandchildren were. Your best friend had her third baby. Your little cousin didn't ask you to be a bridesmaid, and you knew it was because you were so much older than all her friends. The new men at the office dated the seventeen-year-old receptionist, and the men you used to date when you were young, five years ago, were all married by now. And you knew that it was now or never — if you weren't married by the time you were twenty-six, your chances of ever marrying were very slim indeed.

Society has changed radically in this respect. Both men and women can be much freer to develop alternative life styles — to live together without marriage, perhaps, or to postpone making any serious commitment until later in life.

Sooner or later, however, most Americans do get married. Those who do it sooner — in their teens or very early twenties — are the most likely to wind up in the divorce court.

Growing up together

If you're a teenager, you're even more likely than your elders to marry for the wrong reason. With all those teenage hormones going for you, it's easy to think you're in love. And once you're in love, why not get married?

Because you're very likely to regret it, that's why not. You're cutting off most of your other options — education, career, even simple friendships — if you marry too early. Why, then, do so many teenagers do it?

Getting away

You may want to get away from a bad home situation, or one you see as bad. Well, if you think it's tough to be asked to empty the dishwasher before you eat the lunch your mother has fixed, wait until you get married and discover that neither you nor your spouse is really turned on by washing dishes. Or clothes. Or by cooking, dusting, or making beds. One of the unpalatable facts of married life is that you can't spend all your time making love. One of you is going to have to make that bed before you can lie in it.

You may think marriage is a good way to separate yourself from your family, to find a new identity as Bob's wife rather than Harold and Julia's daughter (it's still not common for a young man to think of himself *primarily* as Jane's husband). The trouble with this approach is that being Bob's wife is not an all-consuming job, and so you are going to turn into a pretty warped person if you see yourself only in the reflection in Bob's eyes. You have to find out who you are yourself; sooner or later you're going to be unsatisfied playing the part that Bob has created for you.

Daddy's girl and mama's boy

You may get married because you are looking for a mother or father substitute — either somebody as much like your parent as possible, or as different as you can manage if you weren't crazy about your own real parent.

This may work out for awhile, as long as your spouse is looking for a child, but very few people are willing to be a parent to their marriage partner forever. Even if your spouse is willing to keep playing that role, *you* may want to grow up some time, and you may find it almost impossible to get your partner to let you do it.

Who am I?

If you and your partner are both very young, if neither of you has a good solid sense of identity as yet, you'll have to be very lucky indeed if you still like each other, much less love each other, ten years from now. You need time to get to know yourself — your own strengths and weaknesses, your own talents and ambitions — before you commit yourself to somebody else.

The years between seventeen and twenty-five bring enormous changes to almost everybody. Your life style is likely to change more than it ever has before: you may move away from your parents' home to a college dormitory, or you may get a job and rent an apartment. Even if you have been a reasonably independent and self-propelled kid, you may find that it's quite a shock to realize that the back-up system you've always counted on has now been removed — or at least become less automatic.

You have to budget your own time and your own money. Your mother's car isn't available when your own suddenly breaks down on the way to work. Your father's checkbook is in the house where you don't live any more. Whether you are still involved in getting more formal education, or whether it's on-the-job training, you are engaged in separating yourself from your family.

You are also engaged in defining your own personality, finding out who you are. Families have a way of pigeonholing kids, somehow, unconsciously defining this one as 'the smart one,' that one as 'the athletic one,' another as 'the clumsy one' or 'the pretty one' or

84

'the musical one.' You are likely to find, when you're on your own, that you are both more and less than your family's perception of you. You may not be as bright as everybody in your class, but you're also not as clumsy as your family made you feel. It's hard work (but interesting!) developing your own identity. That identity will change somewhat during your whole life, but the really big jump is in these important formative years of your late teens and early twenties.

By the time you're in your middle twenties, you're likely to be incredulous when you think of the things you liked to do, the people you preferred to be with, the values you had — in short, the person you were — when you were seventeen. If you marry young, you're likely to be even more incredulous when you look at the person you chose to share your life with.

If you are a girl, you may be playing Cinderella or perhaps Sleeping Beauty, believing that marriage is the last task in your development. Once that knight in shining armor shows up, your life will fall into place, and the whole meaning of existence will be in polishing up that visor and keeping him on his white horse, fighting those dragons for you.

This does not work.

It is your job, whether you are male or female, to define your own role, to get to know *yourself,* before you take up with somebody in a relationship you want to be permanent.

Now, this is not to say that if you marry young, you are necessarily doomed. Both John and Jeanne married at twenty-one, are still with their original spouses, and nobody concerned has any intentions of changing partners. Both marriages have had their ups and downs. All marriages do. We have been lucky in our timing. That is, while the alluring stranger and the different life style have appeared on the horizon now and then, they have not happened to coincide with a period of great frustration or discontent within our marriages.

That much is luck. More important — much more important — John and Jeanne and their respective partners have a strong sense of commitment. It takes two, not only to *get* married, but to *stay* married. (More about that in another chapter).

Bolstering your sense of self-worth

Knowing that you are Number One, *the* most important person in the world, to somebody, is a very heady experience. There's nothing wrong with enjoying it, either. Just make sure it isn't the *only* reason you're choosing that particular partner.

If your own sense of self worth is a bit shaky, it can be enhanced quite a bit by knowing that somebody else thinks you're the answer to his or her dreams. But will this happy state of affairs continue once the rosy romantic glow fades? It *will* fade, you know; you may grow, over the years, to love each other more and more deeply, but that falling-in-love feeling is transitory, and sooner or later reality is going to play a bigger part in your mutual concerns.

Right now your partner fills the empty parts in your life; you both feel so good when you're together that neither of you cares what the rest of the world thinks. This is fine. But will it last? That depends. If you are going through a *temporary* period of confusion or self-doubt and your partner demonstrates faith in you, that's great.

John's marriage is a good illustration of that kind of thing: when he got married, he was beginning graduate school, with six years ahead before he could start to support a family. Judy was a real helpmate —

she was willing to keep her job and to encourage him to finish school whenever he had moments of feeling that he really should be doing more to provide their income. That is a positive, helpful kind of faith in your partner.

However, if you are in a situation like that of the mythical client whose therapist told him, "No, you don't have an inferiority complex, Mr. Smith; you really *are* inferior!" — if you are in the wrong field, for instance, or if for some other reason you never do develop your own solid sense of self-worth, your spouse is going to get pretty tired of propping you up all the rest of your life together. That life together may — for that reason alone — be quite brief or quite unhappy.

The key word is *temporary*. If you do not develop your own sense of self-worth, your partner cannot do it for you.

Money

"It's just as easy to fall in love with a rich man as a poor man," said somebody's mother. That may be true, but it is also unfortunately true that if you marry way up or way down the social scale you're likely to have more problems than if the two of you have reasonably similar backgrounds. Far be it from us to suggest that you should let social prudence govern your every action — especially an action as important as choosing a life partner — but you should know that you're going to have built-in problems with any mixed marriage — whether the mix is racial, religious, or monetary.

If you are female and you have the money, your husband is going to have identity problems unless he is a very strong, independent, and preferably creative man. If he can be himself as a sculptor, writer, choreographer or whatever, then your money will simply be a pleasant convenience and he can love you for yourself alone. But if his identity when you fell in love with him was captain of the college (or even worse, high school) football team, and if he hasn't found another identity, you're in trouble.

If you are male and you have the money, this may work out if your wife is socially adaptable and the circles you move in are not too hidebound. Society still has fairly rigid double standards when it comes to marrying for money; it is much more acceptable for a woman to marry a rich man than for a man to marry a rich woman.

Money — whether you have lots by anybody's standards or just quite a lot more than your partner is used to — means control, for the one with the money, and economic dependence, for the one without it.

If you are the one without the money, could you support yourself if you had to? This is a tricky question, especially for women. You may have a bright shiny new degree and be able to answer a confident "Of course!" You'd be surprised how tarnished that degree will look in ten or twenty years, if you can't keep polishing it.

In fact, this question of self-support is tricky whether or not there's lots of money involved. Let's face it, if you take a decade or two out to raise children or be the perfect corporate wife or spend your time on volunteer activities, you may find it hard to get back into the job market again if you need to. Almost half the marriages in America end in divorce. People, even young people, do die, leaving widows or widowers, sometimes with young children. Try to have a few alternatives in mind in case you *don't* live happily ever after.

Giving the baby a name

Oddly enough, in this age of sex education and available contraception, a fair number of young women, especially very young ones, get married

88

because they discover they are pregnant. Some of them get pregnant — deliberately or in a sort of conspiracy with their unconscious feelings — because they want to get married. Some are astonished to find that unwanted pregnancies don't happen only to other people. Some are looking forward to having a sort of live doll, a step up from the plastic ones they were playing with a year or two earlier.

You should not get married *just because* a baby is on the way, if you can find any other solution at all. You have a responsibility not to get pregnant, or not to get your partner pregnant. But if it does happen, you must consider what is best for all three of you — you, your partner, and the coming child.

Marriage carries with it an implicit assumption that it is a relationship between two adults, not between two children. In spite of the sentimental twaddle about 'growing up with your children,' it is really very hard on a baby to have parents who are themselves barely out of childhood. Of course it's hard to give a baby up for adoption; but it is likely to be a lot better for the baby than keeping it if you are getting married only because that baby is on the way.

It's better if you already contemplate marriage, and the pregnancy just means that you set the date up a bit, but it's still not great. You and your partner need, first, to know yourselves, and second, to come to know each other without the complication of a third person. Marriage is a matter of compromises and of gradually increasing intimacy and understanding. It isn't easy to maintain a good marriage even under the best of circumstances; and an instant threesome is far from the best of circumstances.

Marrying on the rebound

You may get married because you need a sense of

security, of stability, and you may need this particularly after you have suffered a dislocation in your former life — such as breaking up with another lover. Whether your bruised ego makes you turn to somebody else in simple gratitude, or whether there's an element of "I'll show her I can find somebody," this situation is hard both on you and on your new partner. Try to wait until you have recovered from your old love before you begin a new one — or at least before you commit yourself in marriage.

So what are you supposed to do?

Marriage is a commitment, a promise to share your love, your troubles, your successes and failures — your life — with each other. It is one of the most rewarding experiences you'll ever have, or it can be. It is also one of the most difficult to sustain. If you have the wrong partner, if you grow in different, antagonistic directions, it can be the source of exquisite misery. If you have the right partner, if you can stay loving, caring, sharing, it can be the source of exquisite pleasure.

Choose carefully.

What do you expect of marriage? What does your partner expect? How are you going to feel about your partner when you're no longer dazed by the first raptures of love? What is he or she really like? For that matter, what are you really like? Humans, when courting, have a natural tendency to be a little nicer than they really are, so to speak — but you can't sustain that level forever. Nobody can. How much mutual disillusionment can you take, and how much mutual tolerance can you come up with?

Try to see through that rose-colored fog into yourself and into your potential spouse's self; be as honest as you can — and try to keep your balance!

*Until Death or
Incompatibility Us Do Part*

Until Death or Incompatibility Us Do Part
(Staying Married)

Four out of ten American marriages now end in divorce, and the rate is rising. You can, of course, turn this around: six out of ten couples stay in their marriage until one of them dies, in which case the survivor probably goes out and gets married again.

Still, four out of ten . . .? Why is this happening?

You should live so long

A hundred years ago, as you can see by visiting any old graveyard, people's lives, especially women's lives, were generally much shorter than they are today. Women would marry at eighteen or twenty, have thirteen children, of whom some survived, and die before they were fifty. Antibiotics, improved nutrition, and birth control have doubled the span of a "till death us do part" marriage, as well as profoundly changing the circumstances of marriage.

When you were raising a dozen children, you didn't have much time for brooding about whether you and your spouse were really communicating with each other; you felt lucky if you had time for a few hasty words together at breakfast. Men worked twelve-hour days, and women worked longer ones. By the time the average woman fixed breakfast for twelve, packed her husband's lunch pail, mended everybody's underwear, got the older ones off to school with their lunch pails, fed the chickens, collected the eggs, nursed the baby a few times, and patted the fevered brows of the three who had chicken pox, it was time to start thinking about dinner. Simply surviving under those circumstances took all the psychic energy she had. No matter how romantic her courtship might have been, she and everybody else understood that marriage implied children — lots of children — and their interests and illnesses were her primary concern. Maybe she loved her husband, maybe she didn't; probably she hardly ever thought about it.

Her husband's work day was no bed of roses either. Twelve hours a day, six days a week, he was laying bricks or making cabinets or driving a carriage. If he could count on coming home to a good hot meal, he was not about to berate his wife for not "growing along with him."

If they both survived until the children were grown, along came the grandchildren, another common bond, and another distraction.

Most Americans, in other words, were simply too busy doing the work involved in raising a family to consider questions of personal fulfillment, even if they lived longer than most people did in those days.

Even if they turned out to be miserable together, they probably stayed married until one of them died. What else could they do? Very few wives could earn enough money to support their children; very few husbands knew how to do the physical work around the house, even if they had the time and energy after their long day at work to give it a try.

And of course, the social pressure against divorce was enormous. The church, the state, your neighbors and your family all disapproved. You had to be brave, callous, or both, to abandon spouse and children and start over, and most people simply didn't.

Great expectations

Marriage is no longer an economic necessity. In fact, if you are both earning money and plan to continue doing so, you'll be better off, as far as taxes are concerned, just to live together; if you get married it will cost you, not only for the wedding but for the rest of your lives or until the tax laws are changed.

Marriage is no longer a necessary prerequisite to raising a child. While a child is undoubtedly better off if it is raised by two parents, you can live together if you like each other, or the child can be raised by one parent alone. There are still some raised eyebrows, but far more acceptance than there was even five or ten years ago — perhaps because so many formerly married parents are now single parents.

Marriage is no longer the only way to have a satisfying, ongoing sex life. (Well, naturally, it never was the only way, but nowadays various alternative arrangements are accepted widely. Would you believe that some landlords used to ask to see a marriage license before they would rent to a heterosexual couple?)

Nevertheless, almost all Americans do get married.

So what do they expect to get out of it?

They probably expect far more than any relationship can reasonably be expected to provide. We, the authors, are in favor of marriage, and we think both partners (with a little luck) can probably find more satisfactions within it than without it. However, if you go into marriage expecting your spouse to fill all your needs, to provide all your emotional satisfaction, to be comforting, stimulating, exciting, loving, sexy, relaxing or whatever else you want when you want it, you're in for trouble.

While you are in the first stages of romantic love, this

will work, or almost work, because you are not really seeing another live, fallible human being like yourself; you are seeing your own romantic fantasy draped over a person who can never exactly match it. After the honeymoon is over, you will both have to do some alterations in the pattern. If you can alter your fantasy to get closer to the reality of the person you married, and he or she can do the same for you, you can have a happy marriage. If you try to alter the person to fit the fantasy, or if you get terribly upset every time you notice that your spouse and your fantasy are not quite identical, there are shoals ahead.

Remember that you can survive — you can even be fairly happy — even if all your needs are not being met perfectly by your spouse. Like so much else in this imperfect life, it's a matter of compromise. No one person can realistically be expected to meet even a majority of your needs. You are lucky if you can get most of them met adequately by a small group of relatives and close friends, by the organizations to which you belong and maybe by your employer.

Suppose you like to read books and then talk about them, while your spouse prefers to play bridge. You will be far better off encouraging your partner to join a bridge club while you trade books with a friend whose interests match yours, than you would be if you kept nagging your marriage partner to take an interest in your reading preferences.

"If you loved me, you would . . ." is an unrealistic statement when it comes to avocations. Sure, shared interests are nice, and they strengthen a marriage, and both of you should try once or twice to enjoy skiing, concert-going, bridge, tennis, jogging, or whatever it is that turns the other one on. You probably will find some things you both like to do; you probably will find others that one of you detests and keeps right on detesting.

Don't worry about it; do your thing by yourself or with somebody else. If you try, you can get most of your needs met one way or another, within and without your marriage.

John, for example, needs to get and to give love; his relationship with Judy takes care of that. He can give love to his children and enjoy seeing them change and grow over the years. His marriage gives him a sense of order and predictability, and a continuing identity. He enjoys being responsive to others, and he gets this need met both by his family and in his professional life. He likes to get a response from an audience; teaching, consulting, and talks to civic groups take care of this. He needs a certain amount of privacy, he wants to keep physically fit, and he likes to compete with himself, so he jogs by himself. Part of his self-definition involves creativity, and he expresses that by inventing games (notably "Gone Bananas") and by working on this book.

Jeanne likes cities; Harney doesn't, with the exception of San Francisco. They go on camping vacations together, or to visit his mother, who lives in a small town. Once in awhile they spend some time together in San Francisco. Jeanne goes to Chicago by herself, and thoroughly enjoys it. It's really more fun to go to a natural history museum, a series of art shows, a bunch of secondhand bookstores, or whatever it is you like doing, by yourself than with someone who is there only because he loves you and wants to please you — and is thoroughly bored!

Compromise. Just don't overload your spouse with too many expectations.

The "me" generation

For many people who have grown up in the seventies, the "me" decade, marriage is loaded with expectations of "What's in it for me?" without serious consideration of the other aspect: "What's in it for my partner?" Or to carry that thought a bit farther, "What do I owe to my spouse? Our children? Our parents? Society in general?"

What does society have to do with your marriage? Well, whether you realize it or not, you wouldn't be here without society's help. You survived your first few days with the help of your mother, the nurses at the hospital; you got through the next few years without dying of diphtheria or smallpox because of the vaccines that somebody devised for people like you. Whether you went to public schools or private ones, you did it at somebody else's expense.

You probably can't pay most of these people back directly; you can, however, refrain from jumping into and out of marriage and turning your responsibilities as spouse and parent over to welfare agencies, truant officers, mental health workers, policemen and all the other people who find themselves dealing with the pitiful problems of broken homes.

Commitment

According to recent surveys, people nowadays very rarely behave like Horatio Alger heroes, rising from stock boy to president in the same company. Even professional people often change careers. When you know that your job is likely to be taken over by a computer and your company is likely to be taken over by a conglomerate, it's hard to develop that old sense of commitment to work.

This attitude sometimes spills over into marriage.

And marriage, without a strong sense of commitment, simply will not work.

Every marriage goes through periods where the partners are simply not meshing properly. Now that the kids are in school, he wants to take a long vacation trip without them — a sort of second honeymoon. Now that the kids are in school, she has registered for the courses she needs to complete the degree she deferred when she got married, and can't take time off. Or he is going through a period of soul-searching, wondering if he wouldn't be happier in business for himself, while she feels the risks are simply too great for someone with preschool children.

If you both have a sincere commitment to your marriage you can work things out. If you don't, it's entirely too tempting to change partners and try again. "For better, for worse, richer or poorer, in sickness and in health . . ." The traditional marriage ceremony carries with it the assumption that marriage is not a static thing, and that nevertheless, the couple are committing themselves to each other through all vicissitudes, through the bad times as well as the good.

Should this marriage be saved?

There are two situations when divorce is probably the only solution.

One is a marriage in which there is physical violence. There are people who will say, "I don't really mind if he hits me once in awhile; it shows he really loves me," or "I only slap her if she's really asking for it." If both partners agree, maybe this is all right — for awhile. The trouble is that violence is likely to escalate as time goes on, and extend not only to more severe wife-beating but also to child-beating. Violence does not solve anybody's problems. If you are in a marriage of this kind, get help — and get out.

The other situation is a marriage in which your basic values are incompatible. If your spouse turns out to get his kicks from something which violates your sense of integrity, whether it be sleeping around, or cheating on his income tax, or selling shoddy merchandise to poor people, or padding his expense accounts, or bullying the kids — staying in the marriage is a form of prostitution, and if you possibly can, you should get out of it.

We make it sound easy, don't we — getting out? It is not easy; even if you can manage it financially, it's not easy.

Divorce

If you are contemplating a divorce, think about these facts:

Even a friendly divorce is not very friendly, with rare exceptions — very rare exceptions.

Jeanne knows two couples who did apparently have a very friendly divorce. They all were avid bridge players; they all played bridge together three times a week. After awhile it became clear to all of them simultaneously that they were mismatched; so they simply switched partners. After the divorces and remarriages, they went right on playing bridge together. When the daughter (stepdaughter) got married, both her mother and her stepmother helped plan the wedding; both worked on her wedding dress. Her real father walked down the aisle with her, and both he and her stepfather were in the reception line.

What her parents and her stepparents didn't know was that right before and right after the divorce (which happened when she was seven or eight) she had recurrent nightmares: her parents' faces kept dissolving and turning not only into faces of strangers, but faces of monsters. She had, after the divorces and remarriages, a brother and a stepbrother, both named George. She lived with her mother but kept her father's last name. The adults came out of this very happily; Jeanne's friend had problems which took years to overcome. She has a master's degree in psychology, and she became interested in the field because of her own special problems.

To take the simplest possible basis for a 'friendly' divorce: suppose you have been married about five years and you have no children; you are both working, and your salaries are reasonably comparable. You live in an apartment. You decide, more or less at the same time, that you just aren't in love with each other any more, that you are getting bored with living together. You want to split and begin again with somebody else known or unknown; no hard feelings on either side.

The question of custody of children doesn't arise. But who gets the dog, which you have had since he was a puppy and which is attached to both of you? Who gets the silver platter from Cousin Emily? She is your cousin, but she made it plain that her treasured platter was going to you only because your choice of marriage partner was so pleasing to her? How do you split the record collection? The photograph album? Is that table really worth as much as the rocking chair?

You *will* find yourselves arguing about trivia such as this when you break up housekeeping, and no matter how friendly you were at the beginning, you're going to be cool, if not positively hostile, by the time you're through.

If you have been married longer, if you are buying a house, and especially if you have children, things are far more complicated.

In most cases, a house, or the equity in a house, is the biggest single asset a couple owns. Quite often, she gets the house, and the children, and he gets the bank account. The book value looks even, or perhaps even slanted in her direction. What nobody seems to give enough consideration to is the fact that a bank account never needs a new roof, or a paint job, or a replacement for the old water heater. Nobody has to clean it or cut its grass. If it has an old mortgage, it's cheaper to stay in the house than to sell it and move to a smaller place; but old as the mortgage is, it's still *there*, demanding its place in the budget. Even if you own the house free and clear, there are taxes and repairs to think about.

Very few couples can manage to maintain the standard of living for two households which they had when they were sharing one.

So much for the financial aspects of divorce. There are far heavier costs involved in any divorce.

The psychic price

When you get a divorce, you are negating the part of your psychic energy that went into your marriage. You must now convince yourself that that five or ten or thirty years was not worthwhile; you have in essence lost that period of time from your own life. You must now devalue what you once valued. What does this do to your self-esteem?

A popular table of stressful events lists divorce as second only to death of a spouse. Perhaps divorce should come first. In most cases, people can't help dying. If your spouse dies, you will, since you are human, have to cope with loneliness, guilt, anger, grief. If you are divorced, whether it is you or your spouse who has initiated it, you will have to cope with all of these — plus a sense of failure, and perhaps of rejection.

You may conclude that divorce is the only way out of a desperate situation; you may well be right. Just be sure that you don't go into it lightly: most of those apparently lighthearted swingers you see around are really more heavy-hearted than you would guess.

Divorce brings depression. The degree of depression, and the length of time it goes on, are dependent on the degree of your former involvement in your marriage.

Divorce brings anxiety. You have lost your old identity, or at least that part of it which was involved in your marriage, and you must begin again. Do you really want to begin the dating, the game-playing, the search for another partner? Most divorced people do search for another partner, if not another marriage partner, at least for somebody with whom they can have a degree of intimacy, of sharing, of caring; the very things they used to have in marriage.

Maybe it is no longer possible to have those things with your original partner; but you both owe it to yourselves to make very certain that your marriage is doomed before you take that final step.

Why are you doing this?

Many of John's clients don't seem able, when they first consult him about a possible divorce, to come up with anything more specific than, "Well, I just feel like it. . . we can't talk to each other any more. . . I'm tired of responsibility; I want to have some fun before it's too late."

Psychology is sophisticated enough today to come up with more specific reasons than that. If you are considering divorce, or even thinking vaguely that your marriage ought to be more interesting, more satisfying, than it is, you ought to get professional counselling. If your spouse thinks it's a good idea, come together; if your spouse thinks it's silly, you come, anyway, alone if need be.

Whether or not you can salvage your present

marriage, it is vitally important for you to know what went wrong. If you don't know, you are very likely to make the same mistakes all over again in your next marriage. People do, somehow, tend to marry the same kinds of people once, twice, three times . . . . If things are to be better for you the second time around, you need to be quite clear about who you yourself are, what your dreams are, and what sort of person will fit well with you.

Separation

Moving out may help you to get some helpful perspective on your floundering marriage. Separation implies a less committed state than marriage. You can see how you like living alone, or alone with your children. You can try getting back into the social world of singles rather than couples. You may find a new sense of freedom and self-confidence, and use it to come back into your marriage with different attitudes and expectations. You may decide you like the single life so well that you want to get a divorce and never get married again. You may hate the whole thing. You'll never know until you try. There is, of course, always the chance that you and your spouse are having different reactions to separation: your spouse may want to leave permanently just as you decide you want to come back together permanently. That's the chance you both have to take. Separation is a chance worth taking if you are considering divorce.

How do you keep a good thing going?

What are those six out of ten couples doing right? Sometimes, nothing much; they are just staying together out of pure inertia, fright, or impossible financial circumstances.

More often, however, they are working on keeping

their marriage not only tolerable, but comfortable, exciting, romantic, or whatever they both think a marriage should be. Or at least, what the most committed partner thinks a marriage should be; no matter how hard you try to communicate and to feel with each other, there are bound to be differences in what each partner thinks is right and wrong in a marriage.

Respect

This is perhaps the most important ingredient in any recipe for a happy marriage. You can disagree, you can have diverse interests and priorities, you can be baffled by your partner's actions: but you must respect each other. This means you must not nag your partner to be more like you, you must allow him or her to choose activities that might be different from your choices, you must not assume that the work you are doing is more important than the work your spouse is doing (or vice versa, for that matter; self-respect is part of this equation, too). In a good marriage, both partners feel good about themselves (not all the time, of course; no marriage is perfect, just as nobody is perfect — we all, unfortunately, are only human) and about each other. Each of them tries to please the other most of the time.

The business of pleasing each other is a two-way street; you must try to please each other, and you must try to be pleased by the other. Sometimes this is not easy. If you have been mentioning for two weeks before your birthday how much you like a given perfume, and on your birthday you get an electric knife sharpener, you have reason to feel that your husband has not been listening to you with that exquisite attention which you deserve. On the other hand, think! — have you ever expressed a passing desire for an electric knife sharpener? Ever? It may be that your husband is not one for the quick fix, so to speak; that it takes months for a gift suggestion to sink into his mind, find some fertile soil, and take root there. Cheer up; Valentine's Day will be here before you know it.

Jeanne remembers (Jeanne will never forget!) one evening years ago. Her husband's parents were expected early the next morning for a two-week stay; Jeanne and Harney had only been married four or five years, and she was still inclined to get a little uptight about visits from in-laws. She had spent the last several days cleaning, polishing, rearranging furniture, and trying to remember what Harney's parents liked to eat. She came downstairs from putting the three preschoolers to bed, to find Harney in the living room, sanding disc in hand. "There," he said delightedly, coated with fine sawdust, as was everything else in the room, "I remembered you wanted me to sand that table; and now I've done it." We will, as a Victorian novelist would put it, draw a veil over the rest of the evening. The fact that Jeanne and Harney, twenty years later, are still married, indicates that though the path of true love may seldom run smoothly, it does tend to dig a channel out for itself, given a little help. Gather up your reserves of goodwill, and assume, unless evidence to the contrary is absolutely overwhelming, that your partner is doing the same for you.

Communication

This is going to get a chapter all of its own, so we will touch on it only very lightly here. John believes that about 60% of communication is nonverbal, while Jeanne thinks that figure is somewhat overstated, unless you count sleeping together (even literally just *sleeping* together). You may get more rest in a single bed, but it isn't nearly as much fun, or as comforting, if you've felt at all estranged during the day. Just waking up in the middle of the night to realize that, while you started off rather stiffly, facing away from each other, each on your own side, you are now comfortably, cozily entwined with each other, makes up for a lot of the "I never will understand what she (he) means by . . ." situations that are bound to come up now and then.

Communication of any sort has to be timed right, and it can be overdone: take the story of the husband and wife, both avid golfers. They had met on a golf course, they had courted on a golf course, and while they had not been married on one, they spent most of their honeymoon there. One night, he was sleepy, while she felt the urge to have a meaningful communication.

"Darling, do you love me?"

"Yes, of course."

"If I died, would you marry again?"

(Long, sleepy pause). "Yes, I suppose maybe I would."

"Would you play golf with her?"

"Well, yes, I guess I would. I know I would."

(Long, rather hurt pause). "Would you let her use my clubs?"

"Oh, no, I wouldn't do that . . . She's left-handed."

Keeping romance in your marriage

You don't have to bring your wife flowers on your anniversary. It's very nice if you do, it couldn't hurt, she will probably be pleased. Anniversaries, birthdays, special occasions are great ways to keep saying, "I'm still glad we found each other."

On the other hand, many a man has bought his wife a diamond bracelet for Christmas and announced in January that he was leaving to find his real self and he hoped she wouldn't be unreasonable about a property division.

Nor do you have to greet your husband, when he comes home for dinner, wearing nothing but a frothy negligee and a great big smile. Romantic little dinners are nice, too, if you really want to do them. If you are just using those candles and that bottle of champagne to soften him up because you want a mink stole or even a new dishwasher, you are being manipulative.

What you are supposed to be, in a good marriage, is honest. Kindly, full of goodwill, wanting to please your partner as much as you can, but (within reasonable bounds of tact and politeness) honest.

Marriage is for intimacy, for sharing, for caring, for feeling that your husband or your wife is really important to you. Not important as a means of financial support (although that may be part of it) or a housekeeper (although that may be part of it) or the parent of your child (although that may be part of it) but primarily as a separate, worthwhile, lovable person.

Everybody, just by being human, is so extraordinarily complex and contradictory, that you can retain that feeling of recurrent surprise which is the essence of romance — just by paying attention — just by seeing your spouse as the human being he or she really is.

Friendly, unreasonable, assertive, submissive, intelligent, willfully obtuse, reliable or as flighty as a weathervane — but a unique, irreplaceable human being. Just as you are.

Just You and Me, Babe!

Just You and Me, Babe!

(Attachment)

Timmy doesn't remember his real mother at all. He doesn't remember the neighbor whose exasperation at the thin wailing that came through the apartment wall day and night for weeks turned to horror when she finally called the police, who broke in to find Timmy lying on the floor — cold, wet, hungry, and completely alone. Timmy's mother, who had been deserted by his father a couple of months before Timmy was born, was picked up at a local disco.

"What do you mean you're charging me with child neglect and abuse? Sure, I hit the kid once in awhile; how else could I get him to eat his cereal? And, God, he used to drive me up the wall with his crying sometimes — never any peace night or day. Yeah, I left him alone tonight; what the hell, I was only gonna be gone a couple hours. I've gotta have *some* fun, you know."

Timmy doesn't remember the police who took him to the hospital, or the doctors and nurses who patched up his broken ribs and his broken arm, and kept him warm and dry and fed until he gained three pounds. After all, he was only six months old when all this was happening to him.

He doesn't remember anything about the earliest foster homes, either. He lived in thirteen different foster homes during his first nine years — some for only a week or two, some for almost a year. Of course, he remembers the more recent ones: the McGraths,

111

who were warm and loving and kept him for three months, until Mr. McGrath had a fatal heart attack and Mrs. McGrath went back to live with her parents, who didn't like little kids. Then there were the Johnsons, who had three other foster children. They turned him out after two weeks, because he wet his bed one night. And the Murrays, who had him for almost a year before they gave up.

"That boy," said Mrs. Murray, "is impossible to put up with. He lies; he steals; he runs away; he skips school. Well, goodness knows I tried. But I caught him one day putting a pillow over the baby's head — trying to suffocate her is what he was doing. Well, I couldn't keep him any longer after that. That boy doesn't have any trust or love in him, and God only knows what's going to become of him."

Timmy is eleven now, and he has been living in a group home for emotionally disturbed children for the past two years. The staff thinks he's getting better: he doesn't disrupt classes or meals now nearly as often as he once did; he's learning to read, although he is still well below his normal grade level, and he is even beginning to get along better with the other children.

The consulting psychologist notices that Timmy never makes eye contact with anyone; he looks over the shoulder or at the feet of anyone he's talking to.

To Timmy, all the Rorschach blots are pictures of monsters. He dreams of monsters, too, huge dragons with claws to snatch him up and wings to carry him away.

The psychologist gives him a sentence-completion test:

"When I am grown up I would like to . . . " "Be Superman," says Timmy. "I think girls are . . ." "Bad." "I think boys are . . . "Bad." "My mother is

112

. . ." "I don't know." "If I went to a desert island, the one person I'd like to have with me is . . ." "Everybody." "Just *one* person." "I don't know, nobody, I guess."

Timmy is an unattached child.

He is full of fear, hatred, and bitterness. He has learned in his short lifetime that you can't trust people, that if you do something bad — or maybe even if you don't — they will send you away. It's safer not to try to get close to anybody. If you don't make friends in the first place, you can't lose them. If you run away, or throw food in the lunchroom, or have a tantrum in school, you are showing the grownups in your life that you — not they — are the one in charge. And how can you trust *any* grownup to be in charge of your life? They've sure messed it up so far.

Timmy may some day be able to trust and to love somebody. More likely, he never will: the damage is done, and the psychic scars are too deep. If he has children of his own, he will probably beat them, just as he was beaten.

It would be surprising if a child with Timmy's background were not emotionally disturbed. But there are children who are much better cared for than Timmy ever was who will also grow up unattached.

There's Melanie, for instance.

Melanie's parents, David and Ruth, met in college. He was majoring in business administration, and she was in her last year of nursing school. They planned their joint life very carefully. Both were from divorced families, and had been shunted around among natural parents, stepparents, and step-stepparents. None of that for them! They were going to wait until they were quite sure of each other, and until they both had finished their education. Then they would get married,

113

work a few years in their chosen professions, and then, perhaps in five years, when David had been promoted a time or two, Ruth would take a leave of absence and have a child.

The first year of their marriage worked out just as they had hoped. David was on the lowest rung of the ladder at the local bank, and Ruth worked as an operating room nurse. Their joint income was enough to pay for an attractive apartment, and they even managed to save a little money.

And then — somehow — Ruth found she was pregnant. As the months went on, their initial dismay turned to resignation, and then to pleasure. After all, they had planned to have a child sometime; they had a little money in the bank, and David was about due for a promotion. Maybe the baby would even help — banks were known to like settled family men as junior officers.

A month before Melanie was born, David was driving home from work when he hit a patch of ice and skidded into an embankment. He lived three days.

Ruth went through the next month in a state of shock. David *couldn't* be dead . . . he *couldn't* have left her to carry out their plans, the plans they had made together, all by herself.

When Melanie was born, Ruth found herself taking a dim kind of clinical interest in the process, listening to the other nurses saying the same sort of thing she herself had often said: "The contractions are less than two minutes apart now, doctor; I think perhaps you should come over soon."

Melanie, Ruth realized in a detached sort of way, was a nice normal baby. But without David, she couldn't really get interested in her. Oh, she saw to it that the baby was well taken care of, but all the time she was still mourning David; her energies were concentrated on grieving and on worrying. There wasn't enough insurance, they didn't yet have enough savings. She would have to go back to work. And then what would she do with the baby?

She found the perfect babysitter, a placid, conscientious girl who was studying commercial courses. Nancy turned up promptly at 6:30 every weekday morning and stayed until Ruth got home again at 4:00. Melanie was well fed, clean, warm.

Ruth, after her strenuous shift at the hospital, could relax and stare at the television, or try to concentrate on a book; the baby was usually asleep when she was home.

Nancy spent the days practicing shorthand and studying for the next bookkeeping test. Whenever the baby cried, she fed her, changed her, bathed her. She never cuddled her or played with her. And neither did Ruth.

Neither of the women noticed that Melanie never smiled. How could she learn to smile, when nobody smiled at her?

Melanie may well grow up to be another unattached person. She's young enough, at six months, to have another chance. If Ruth finishes her grieving, if she finds a babysitter who enjoys playing with babies — if somebody cuddles Melanie and plays with her — Melanie will be all right. The human race has survived because most adults enjoy playing with babies, most mothers instinctively cuddle their infants, smile at them, talk to them. And the babies smile back.

Timmy and Melanie are victims of faulty parenting. Some good parents, however, have babies who simply won't respond to normal methods. What do you do if you pick your baby up and he stiffens and screams? Or if you smile at him and he gazes stonily into the middle distance, as though the sight of your friendly face is too revolting to contemplate?

Well, first you make sure that he doesn't have a physical problem. Can he really see? Can he hear?

And then you stop blaming yourself. Some babies are just like that. What you have to do is *insist* on holding him and talking to him. Eventually, he will relax and begin to respond to you. It may take a long while — don't give up. This kind of baby is not easy to like, but he's yours, and you have to do the best you can with him and for him.

If your child is beyond babyhood, how do you tell if he or she is unattached? An unattached child will be reluctant to look you in the eye, won't want to be touched, will be prematurely autonomous. Is there such a thing as a child who is too independent too soon? Isn't self-reliance and independence something every parent wants for every child — the sooner the better?

Not quite. A child who is attached to a parent, who can trust the adult world to take good care of him, will indeed become independent and self-reliant at the proper time. But a child should go from trust in adults or at least one other adult to trust in himself. Skipping that first step — trust in a parent — leads to mistrust not only of other adults but also of himself. He may act independent, but he is really unsure and unhappy; he has no guidelines to help him in the world he's trying to understand.

If you do have an unattached child, remember that it isn't necessarily your fault. Perhaps you were ill or had to be away too much — perhaps you were right there, loving and caring, and the child for one reason or another didn't *perceive* you as being there in the way he wanted you to be. Whatever the cause may be, if you have an older unattached child, hang in there — it's important for you, your child, and society in general to try to form an attachment. Do a lot of hugging and cuddling, even if your child doesn't want you to. Insist that he pay attention to you when you talk, that he answer you when you ask a question, that he look you in the eye. (Again, check with an eye specialist first; if your child is very farsighted, he *can't* focus in close enough to look you in the eye unless you are across a large room!)

If none of that works, try a psychologist (we don't mean to suggest that you should only consult psychologists when you're desperate, but this business of attachment is something that should take place between parent and child, and if you really work at it, you can probably make it happen).

Suppose both parents have to work outside the home. Are you necessarily going to have an unattached child? Not if your primary caretaker — whoever it is who is with the child most of the time — is good. In the old-fashioned 'normal' family where the father earned the money and the mother stayed home and took care of the children, the children's first attachment would usually be to the mother. It doesn't have to be, just so the child has some one person to love and trust in the first year or year and a half.

If you have to be away from your baby more than you'd like to, you can still see to it that the time you do spend together is good. For instance, don't prop a bottle in the crib; hold the baby during feeding times. You can catch up on a lot of reading or television or record listening this way; the baby won't care whether you're gazing into his eyes all the time — the most important thing is the feeling of your warm arms. You can smile at him during commercials or while you change his diapers. It really doesn't take that much extra time or effort — and the effect on your child can be enormous.

A child who has never become attached to anyone in his or her early years will have trouble making friends or forming any kind of close, enduring relationship — with you or anybody else. He won't want to please you — and if you've never tried coping with a child who doesn't care to please you, you have no idea how impossible that situation can be! Out of simple self-preservation, as well as concern for your child, you'd better try as hard as you can to foster attachment.

Now suppose that you have done all the right things and your baby has seemed to be rather fond of you. Then he has his second birthday, and suddenly you are both plunged into the 'Terrible Twos.' Does this mean something has gone wrong with the attachment process? No. Attachment takes place in the first year to year and a half; after that your child wants to move on — indeed, should move on — to the next phase of development: experimenting with independence, disagreeing with you just to see if the sky will fall in if he does. It's not the most pleasant year to be a parent, but it's interesting, and things get better pretty soon. Or at least different.

Most parents who have read Spock or Gesell or any other child expert automatically brace themselves as their child nears its second birthday. However, some parents suddenly realize that Junior is now three or four and is just as placid and agreeable as ever. Is this bad? It depends. There are some children who stay dependent too long; there are others who manage to be polite and friendly while trying their wings.

One of the authors (Jeanne) had two bright, early-talking girls. As they began approaching what appeared to be the age of reason, she would lead them around the house, saying, "Now this you do *not* touch — ever — because it is (hot, breakable, heavy) — this you be gentle with, because if you aren't, it will scratch you or bite you. . ." Those kids never destroyed a book, a record, a plant, or a cat. Of course, the house (except for books, records, plants, and cats, none of which could be put out of reach) was pretty well child-proofed: no poisons at low levels, safety covers on the electric outlets, pot handles turned away from the stove front. The girls simply never acted like your stereotyped two-year-old; they had adventures but they never had a tantrum; they began making more of their own decisions, but they used such good judgment that they rarely had a run-in with their mother.

Then the third child arrived: a 2½ lb. boy who spent his first three months in an incubator. When he eventually became mobile, he chewed on the plants, the books, the records, the telephone cord, and the cat. Words apparently meant nothing at all to him — he did what he wanted to do when he wanted to do it, and no amount of reasoning, coercion, or diversion had any effect on him. It took about five years to reach any real rapport with him.

Well, at this point, they're all young adults, and they're all doing well.

In other words — hang in there, don't depend too much on the experts, and everything is more likely than not to come out more or less all right — as long as you have an appropriate attachment between you and your child.

The wrong kind of attachment

One of John's first patients was a sixteen year old girl who had been hospitalized for schizophrenia. Her father was about forty, and a highly sexed man. He felt his wife was hostile and unloving, and he spent more and more of his time in his basement workshop. The daughter took to coming downstairs wearing only a robe, and behaving quite provocatively. One thing led to another, and they made love over a period of a good many months.

Finally, the daughter simply retreated from reality into schizophrenia — it was the only way she could escape her guilt and anxiety. Every time the subject was brought up she became confused. Her fantasy was that Prince Charming would turn up some day soon, and take her away from this unbearable situation.

We are using this case history because it may typify what people believe about incest: that it is due to a wife's coldness, that the child provokes the relationship, that the girl involved is in her middle teens. Actually, it is not typical of most incestuous relationships. Incest is most likely to occur between brothers and sisters; the next most common relationship is between stepfathers and step-daughters; incest does not necessarily involve inter-course; and the girls are usually considerably younger than sixteen. Reliable statistics are hard to come by, since incest does not tend to be reported by the victim, but some studies indicate that the average age of the child is thirteen, while others put it at eight for the beginning and eleven or twelve for the end of a typical incestuous relationship.

Mother-son incest does exist, but it is apparently extremely rare; as far as parent-child relationships are concerned, it is usually the father or stepfather who is the aggressor. The child is usually too young to be deliberately provocative; "This is a secret between you and Daddy," is enough to convince her that everything must be all right, since Daddy, of course, knows best.

How does this twisted sort of attachment begin? Adults need both physical and emotional intimacy. If parents can't get it from each other, one may try to get it from a child. This does seem to be a common denominator in most cases: the father perceives his wife as cold or hostile.

There are cases where a man has had sexual relations with a long series of daughters, beginning with the oldest and working on down the line. Clearly, this sort of man is attracted more to children than to adult women. In the less clear-cut cases, the questions of whether the wife is really hostile or the child is really provocative are irrelevant: the child is the one who will feel guilty; and a child — even a sixteen year old child — should not have to feel guilty about a relationship with an adult authority figure. The guilt should belong to the adult.

How long did John's patient remain schizophrenic? What were her feelings toward men as she grew older? What were her chances for a happy marriage? We don't know. We do know that her prognosis was better than that of a child who has suffered maternal deprivation — by death, indifference, or sheer incompetence on the part of his or her parent.

Letting go

Assuming that you are one of the vast majority who have had a normal attachment between you and your child — how do you untie the apron strings? How do you let go, and how do you encourage the child to let go when the right time comes?

Many primitive societies have puberty rites of some sort; when a boy is old enough to go through the ritual, he is old enough to move away from his parents, emotionally as well as physically. Unfortunately, our society does not provide anything comparable; individual families decide whether they can or will support a child through high school, through college, through years of graduate school, or whether, once children turn eighteen, it's time for them to be up and away.

It is a parent's job, no matter what financial arrangement he may have made, to encourage children to become more independent. This process ought to start early and continue for years; it happens gradually, and can be confusing and sometimes maddening to keep working on, but it is one of the primary tasks of a parent to encourage autonomy in a child. Children who do not become disengaged turn into adults who view the world in a childlike way, who can't take risks or expand their horizons. They question their own judgment, and don't appreciate their own ability to make things turn out to their own satisfaction. We are *not* saying that young adults should abandon their parents; we are not even saying that parental advice is worthless. We are saying that grown children who are too emotionally dependent upon their parents are going to be less fully human than they might be.

Do you still feel that "Mother knows best?" Do your parents mean more to you than your current relationship? Is one of your parents coming between you and your partner? Do you think of "home" as the place where you grew up rather than the place where you are living now? Do you consider, whenever you have to make a major decision, what your parents would think?

If so, you are too dependent upon your parents. It doesn't even matter whether they are still alive. A ghostly vision of Mother's shocked face is a powerful deterrent for many people.

If you think you are still too dependent on your parents — work on it. It's a hard thing to do; you may need professional help. But to begin with, start working on commitment between you and your partner; a warm, solid, real relationship is the best antidote for overdependence on an old, outworn dependency.

Whether you are a parent or a grown-up child — let go! Or prepare to let go. As the author of Ecclesiastes says, "To every thing there is a season, and a time to every purpose under the heaven . . . a time to get, and a time to lose; a time to keep, and a time to cast away . . ." Maybe your time is now.

Who's in Charge Here?

Who's in Charge Here?
(Control)

When you stop to think about it, you'll realize that there are a number of different aspects to the word "control."

There is, for instance, self-control, in the usual sense of behaving more like a normal human being than like an aspirin commercial.

There is the question of which part of your personality is usually in control of your actions.

There is the happy feeling of being more or less in control of your own destiny.

And there is the desire to control other people, or to avoid being controlled by them.

Self-control

A little of this is a good thing, both for you and for the people with whom you come in contact. People with a reasonable degree of self-control are a lot nicer to deal with than those who come apart at the seams in every minor crisis, and of course they live a more pleasant and productive — because less frantic and distraught — life.

However, there is such a thing as too much self-control. Too much self-control gives you a very rigid, unspontaneous, repulsively cold personality. Your life may not be full of unpleasant surprises, but you may also miss all the pleasant unexpected things that most of us enjoy.

If you never — or hardly ever — let yourself scream or laugh or cry, if you never let your emotions rather than your reason take over, you're missing half of life. You may be thought of as a very dependable person. You are also likely to be thought of as a hopeless bore.

Now, we aren't advocating "letting it all hang out" whenever the spirit moves you; but a mentally healthy balance involves both reason and emotion, and emotion which is not just felt but appropriately expressed. It's important to be in tune with yourself. What are you feeling at the moment? If you're angry, why? With whom? Parcel out your anger bit by bit; don't save it all up until you explode. You need a *blend* of reason and emotion; you need to know yourself well enough to realize that, for instance, you are really angry with the buyer who kept you waiting for two hours and then didn't give you the order you expected. Taking your anger out by snarling at your children is not fair.

Jeanne has a fairly placid, easy-going nature, but there were times, when she was dealing with three pre-school children, that took more than a normal ration of placidity. She found that (as long as she used this ploy only on rare occasions) it worked like a charm to line the kids up and say firmly, "I am not feeling at all kindly toward anybody today, and I think you should know that this is *not* the day to yell at each other, or to decorate the coffee table with fingernail polish, or to do *anything at all* that I don't want you to do. I will let you know as soon as I feel better." Young as they were, they seemed to realize that even adults couldn't be expected to have perfect self-control all the time — and they appreciated knowing that it was Mama's mood, and not something *they* were responsible for, that was setting the atmosphere.

Jeanne reciprocated by not being too terribly unrealistic in what she expected of them in the way of self-control. Any parent can tell you that this business of trying to mold those little characters a bit while leaving children some breathing space gets very tricky indeed; it's a wonder that most adults aren't more warped than they are, when you consider what children have to put up with, even from the best-intentioned parents!

So much for self-control as it concerns a balance between reason and emotion.

Self-control also lops sloppily over into what you might prefer to call self-discipline: the whole business of changing habits, cultivating other habits, reaching a life style that is satisfactory to you and to your associates, involves self-control.

The thing here is that it has to be *self*-control. You are not going to stop smoking pot or tobacco, lose thirty pounds, begin walking ten miles a day, keep your house or your desk in perfect order, or write that definitive paper because somebody else wants you to do it.

Not until you, yourself, want to do it.

John once had a client who was a college student. He had a number of psychological problems, but to his father's mind, one of the biggest ones was the fact that he smoked pot. The worried father had read a great deal about marijuana, and one day he and his son came in together to see John. After the father had delivered an eloquent lecture on the deleterious effects of pot smoking, the son said, "I really appreciate what you've been saying, Dad. But if I stop smoking, it's not going to be because you want me to; if I stop it'll be because *I* know it's not good for me."

As you might guess from that comment, the son's

therapy was successful. He eventually took control of his own life, not only in the area of pot smoking, but in more important ones.

Id, Ego, Superego

If you have read the chapter on Freud, you may remember these terms. As we said there, people tend to be more strongly influenced by one or another of these facets of their personality than by the others.

For example, if you are a sort of "normal neurotic" person with a nice uninhibited Id, you wouldn't be our choice for our bookkeeper or our lawyer. On the other hand, you'll always be great fun at a party, although maybe somebody else should drive you home.

People who operate largely from the Id part of their personality give in to their impulses most of the time. This makes them spontaneous and sometimes very charming. On the other hand, people who listen to their Id almost exclusively can't be counted on. A fellow committee member of this kind can drive you right up the wall — he works largely on the pleasure principle, and rarely if ever does a committee report give him pleasure; so he may just put it off forever.

People with an overdeveloped Superego are conscientious and conscience-ridden. They are trustworthy when they have promised to do something for somebody else. On the other hand, they may have an absolutely terrible time making decisions on their own, because they don't want to make a mistake; they want to lead a perfect life. Since they, like the rest of us, are only human, this doesn't work out very well: they can't avoid making mistakes, of course; they just give themselves fits whenever they have to make a decision.

Jeanne has an otherwise delightful friend who does not like to go shopping by herself. She doesn't want to depend on her own judgment, but prefers to consult with somebody as to whether that skirt is too short or that jacket is too loose.

Now, lots of people think of shopping as a social occasion which they want to share with a friend. *This* friend has never snagged anybody into accompanying her more than once, since she is perfectly capable of spending two or three hours trying to decide whether to get the lime green sweater or the burnt orange one. "The green one I could wear with my white dress, you know, the one with the buttons . . . but maybe I couldn't. Do you think the collar would look right? Maybe I should come back tomorrow and wear the dress and see how it looks. No, I can't do that, because they'll probably have sold the sweater by then, it's really a very good buy. I could get it now and take it home and try it, but if I didn't like it I don't suppose they'd take it back, it came from that rack that says "All sales final," didn't it? Now if I got the burnt orange one, I could . . ."

This unfortunate woman is hung up on the weighty problem of buying clothes.

If your Superego is too much in control of you all the time, to the point where you don't dare make a mistake, you may spend equally inordinate amounts of time mulling over alternatives in connection with everything from vacations to restaurants to what color napkins would look best with tonight's centerpiece (assuming you have been able to come up with a centerpiece in the first place; choosing this tulip over that one needs a lot of thought!)

People whose Id and Superego are properly squashed down, not mangled but not encouraged to pop up all the time, are operating mostly through the Ego part of their personality, and they are the ones who are most likely to feel that they have reasonable control over their lives. They can act responsibly toward other people, but at the same time they can save part of their time and energy for themselves. In other words, there's a happy balance between the decision-making and the feeling parts of their personality.

Autonomy

Autonomy — a feeling of independence, of being in control of your own life — is one of the aims of therapy. Actually, of course, you never do have *complete* control over your own life, unless you commit suicide — and even then only if you plan your method with care and perform your execution with great efficiency; it's amazing what modern medicine can do nowadays to revive would-be suicides.

We have, really, very limited control, or at best, partial control over our lives.

You can spend ten years working your painful way up the corporate ladder, only to have some multinational outfit take your company over and replace all of your people with their own people.

You can pay great attention to your health — drink only very moderately, smoke not at all, get all your vitamins and minerals, and greet each dawn by jogging ten miles — and get knocked off by some bleary-eyed motorist who mistook your fluorescent jogging suit for a mirage.

You can follow the advice of your friendly mutual fund salesman and begin socking money away for your children's college education while they are still infants — and discover when the time comes that what would have paid for a bachelor's degree twenty years ago now covers about a semester and a half.

There are times when you have very little control over your own life, when your actions must be adapted to somebody else's needs. If you have a baby, for instance, you must feed it, change it, bathe it, cuddle it; or you must pay somebody else to do that for you (but you'd better be careful who you get; see our chapter on Attachment).

Nevertheless, you can have a *feeling* of autonomy. Presumably you chose to have that baby. Even if you didn't, you can still tell yourself that this part of your life is going to be over pretty soon, that you might as well put up with the scutwork and enjoy the aspects that are fun, and get back to perfecting your bridge game or running your department or whatever it is that turns you on, when the baby is a bit older and less demanding.

Autonomy is largely subjective. You can feel put upon, harassed, pulled about by other people when anybody who looked at your life from outside would say that you had a great deal of freedom. And you can feel autonomous, happy, in control of your own life when an outsider would believe that anyone in your situation must feel frustrated and downtrodden.

Jeanne's mother-in-law is a splendid example of the importance of your attitude. For the last several years of her husband's life, he grew progressively more blind, to the point where he could find his way around the house only by touch, and progressively more forgetful; she would tell him that she was going to a meeting of the library board, and come back in an hour to find him in a panic because he couldn't find her.

So she simply stopped going anywhere. And when anyone commiserated with her on her narrow life, she said, "He's taken care of me for more than fifty years; I'm glad to have a chance to take care of him."

She felt autonomous; she *chose* to give him her constant, loving care.

Everybody wants to feel autonomous. Toddlers, from

the time they are about two years old, are striving for autonomy. Parents have to have enormous amounts of patience to avoid jeopardizing this healthy growth. It's so much easier to say, "You've got the shoes on the wrong feet; let me fix them for you . . . no, you've missed the back of your neck, I'll scrub it for you . . . the fork goes on the *left* and the knife goes on the *right*, you go watch TV and I'll finish setting the table."

When John's daughter Jennie was four or five years old, the family was at the dinner table, and Jennie kept banging her water glass with a spoon. John, having just read Ginott's advice on handling this sort of situation, said gently, "Jennie, that noise is awfully hard on my ears." Bang. Bang. Bang. "Jennie, that really hurts my ears." Bang. Bang. Bang. "Jennie, that noise really bothers me."

At which point Jennie deliberately banged three more times, grinned, and laid down her spoon. She heard what John was telling her, all right, and to a degree she was willing to cooperate with him, but she wanted to choose her time — she needed to feel that she was in control of her own actions.

Even cats apparently like to feel autonomous. Jeanne's family has several of them. The oldest one clearly feels that breakfast should be served at seven o'clock, and that Jeanne is the Cat Food Dispenser. Since Jeanne's husband Harney also feels that breakfast should be served at seven o'clock, this works out pretty well most of the time.

But if Jeanne decides to sleep a little longer, the cat takes control. Harney can be in the kitchen eating, and the cat knows perfectly well that Harney would feed him on request. The cat, however, wants Jeanne to do it; so he jumps onto the bed, carefully pulls the blankets away from her face, and delicately puts one claw out to touch her cheek. This works like a charm, every time: Jeanne's eyes fly open and she leaps out of bed. Jeanne may not be autonomous, but the cat sure is.

Suppose you feel that you're not in control of your own life? Let's say that you have a supervisor who keeps blue-pencilling your reports, a wife who feels that painting the house is your job, not hers, and three small children who want you to read bedtime stories to them for half an hour just when you want to catch the evening news?

Your feeling of helplessness comes from not being able to see any way out. You need your job, you love your wife and children but you feel that they, and not you, are controlling your home life, you don't, in other words, feel that you are controlling your own destiny.

What do you do?

First, you make a mental inventory; stop and reflect upon your life. Get in touch with the Ego — the decision-making part of your personality. Just doing that will help you feel less victimized.

Then you set yourself small, realistic goals. Don't try to reform the world or turn yourself into another person. Stick to small things. A happy byproduct of setting yourself a goal and achieving it is that you will feel more self-worth. If your supervisor keeps objecting to the way you write things up, you could take a short night course in report writing. If your report writing is really all right, and the supervisor just doesn't like you, you could request a transfer to another department, or look for a job with another company, or remind yourself that your idiot boss has only another three years to go to retirement, and that meanwhile you'll have to get your kicks somewhere other than on the job.

You can compromise with your wife on the paint job: you do the sanding and the high parts, and she'll do the low places. You explain to the kids that either you will read them *one* bedtime story and then relax with the paper, or if they will give you half an hour to unwind after supper, you will read them *three* bedtime stories.

The important thing is to start small, start now, and start something at which you know you can succeed.

Controlling other people

For most people, this is a constant temptation. You can see clearly that the girl your brother is dating is all wrong for him, that the motorcycle your old high school buddy just bought is going to keep him broke buying repair parts, and that your wife could get the housework done in half the time if she would just organize things more efficiently.

Shouldn't you give these people the benefit of your valuable insights?

No, you shouldn't.

If someone actually *asks* for your advice, it may be all right to give it to them. But even then, you'd better listen carefully. The woman who says wistfully, "Do you think this new suit is really becoming? I spent more on it than I usually do, but now I'm not sure that this shade of purple is right for me . . ." is not asking for information; she's looking for reassurance. Tell her she looks great. If she's really convinced that she does, she *will* look great, because she'll feel great.

Control can be overt or subtle. Take the husband who expects his wife to do all the cooking for the family, but who wanders into the kitchen while she is putting the finishing touches on dinner and says, "You know, if you kept all the pans together on the *left* shelf here, and put the cups over *there*, and the plates behind them, it would be much easier to find things."

Depending upon the wife's temperament, she may react with belligerence, with deference, or with a reasonable explanation of why she likes things as she has arranged them. In any case, what she's likely to be feeling is something between mild annoyance and blind fury, because her husband is trying to control her. He probably doesn't think of it that way; he's just trying to be helpful.

Parents tend to be particularly obnoxious when it comes to trying to control their children. After all, that's what being a parent is all about, isn't it? If you can't control your kids, how are you going to teach them anything?

What you have to do — and it isn't easy, it's maddeningly difficult — is to let them make their own choices whenever you possibly can. You can't let them choose to run into the street when a car is coming, of course, but you *can* let them choose to wear red shoes instead of blue ones, or have orange juice instead of tomato juice. You can even let them choose to put their homework off until after dinner, or not do it at all, as long as they are old enough to understand that whatever happens at school the next day as a consequence is their responsibility, not yours.

What you have to do constantly, when you are a parent, is examine your own motivation. When you try to control your children, are you doing it for their good, or for yours? Is this situation one where they really need your help — your control — or are you on a power trip of your own? Running your child's life may be very ego-enhancing for you, but pretty tough on the kid.

If you keep taking over a child's problems, you are implying that the child is incapable of making good choices. The longer this goes on, the more likely it is to be true; children who are treated this way will come to feel that any of their decisions are likely to be wrong, and pretty soon will either stop trying to make decisions at all, or will do something drastic like running away from home or taking up with the neighborhood pre-delinquent set.

No human being, not even a parent, should *control* another human being. We all try it, usually with the best of intentions (at least, with the best of *conscious* intentions). And we're all irritated when somebody else tries to control us.

The trouble is, the people we try to control are usually our nearest and dearest — our children, our spouses, our close friends — the people we most want to love us.

Ask yourself, the next time you find yourself trying to control someone else, just what the issue is worth.

You may feel strongly that the toothpaste tube should be rolled from the bottom, not squeezed from the top. If your spouse is a confirmed toothpaste tube squeezer, nagging probably won't help anyway; but if it did, would it be worth it? Which is more important to you, a neat toothpaste tube or a loving mate? Remember, people who feel they are being controlled are too full of resentment to feel very loving.

You may want every light bulb in the house turned off as much as possible. Your children, if they're like most children, are going to skitter gaily from room to room turning lights on, but never off.

What's it worth? You are right, of course: if everybody left all their lights burning all the time, we would be running out of energy even faster than we are already. The children should learn to turn off unused lights. Sooner or later, they will learn.

Meanwhile, what's it worth? If the light bulb situation is turning into a battle for control, if your feeling of power and the children's feeling of power — or lack of it — is centered on a 40-watt bulb, you must ask yourself whether the real issue is power (as in kilowatt hours) or power (as in control).

Remember, in a control battle, there are no winners. Everybody loses. Is that really what you want?

People who feel secure within themselves — who have a good sense of self-worth — don't need to control others. If you find yourself constantly engaged in power struggles, you might ask yourself why. Sometimes you can't avoid them, but if they form the major pattern of your life, ask yourself how you really feel about *you*.

If you are in reasonable control of your own life, you will have far less need to be in unreasonable control of the lives of others.

Anything You Can Do,
We Can Do Better

Anything You Can Do,
We Can Do Better
(Chauvinism)

The term 'chauvinism' comes from one Nicolas Chauvin, a soldier who served under Napoleon I and who was so fanatically devoted to his leader, even when it became clear to everybody else that the empire was definitely defunct, that his bellicose insistence upon the eventual success of Napoleon's venture became an object of derision.

The habit of mind which is described by the term 'chauvinism' is far older than that. Older than the time when certain inhabitants of the Mediterranean basin described themselves as 'Greeks' and everybody else as 'barbarians.' Older than the time when certain inhabitants of the Fertile Crescent decided that raising sheep was better than raising grain (doesn't it shake you a bit, to realize how far back in history range wars extend?) and illustrated their belief with the story of Cain (who was a farmer) and Abel (who was a proper rancher).

Anthropologists have found that primitive tribes tend to call themselves by names which can be roughly translated as something like 'The People,' 'The Ones Who Have Seen the Light,' 'The Good Guys.' All very comforting, no doubt, at times when the harvest is not what one would have wished, or the monsoon season seems to plan to go on indefinitely, or one has just lost the latest skirmish in the latest war.

The first beings to conceive the concept of

chauvinism were probably those proto-humans who decided that the tool-using apes on this side of the river were the *real* people, while those across the stream were mere pale imitations — not really proper simians.

The only trouble with this habit of thought is that if *we* are 'the people,' *you* must be something like 'the-less-than-human;' if *we* are 'the ones who have seen the light,' *you* must be 'the ones who are deliberately travelling in outer darkness;' if *we* are 'the good guys' — what else can *you* possibly be but 'the bad guys'?

Chauvinism runs (like almost anything else in human life) in a spectrum. On the innocent side, it represents the tendency to root for the home team. It serves a useful function in making a group of people feel like a team, a tribe, a community.

On the less innocent — the dark—side, it leades to lynchings, witch-burnings, war.

The insidious thing about chauvinism of any kind is that it is usually at least partially unconscious. Chauvinists make assumptions about groups other than their own (and of course about their own group, too) which they then internalize to the point where they would be astonished if anyone in the world were to contradict them. The groups on the 'out' or 'down' side of chauvinism sometimes internalize the same convictions. Think of all the women who are against the Equal Rights Amendment. Think of all the Negro leaders who urged their people, after the Civil War, to become skilled in manual arts, or to work hard at unskilled labor (although that may have been realism — where are the jobs likely to be? — rather than a conviction that their group could not handle intellectual tasks as well as white men could). No woman, of course, could be a scholar.

Chauvinism exists whenever any group (males,

whites, females, blacks, Hispanics, Arabs, Americans
. . .) believes that it has The Truth, that it has more
competence than the opposing group, that it deserves
to have its present place in the sun (which is likely to be
a more pleasant piece of real estate than the out group,
whoever it is, is presently enjoying).

Chauvinism fits in with the human tendency to
classify things by making certain classifications very
simple indeed: All black people are lazy, fond of
watermelon, and inclined to have a better sense of
rhythm than white people. You notice that chauvinism
can extend to admirable traits — surely a sense of
rhythm is a good thing? However, we have known
blacks who won't even *try* to dance or play drums
because they are so tired and resentful of that
particular stereotype.

Everyone needs a sense of power, of mastery, of
control over one's life — although until very recently,
this need was socialized out of women: women were
supposed to derive their highest level of fulfillment by
nurturing their men and their children, and basking in
the reflected glory of *their* achievements.

Chauvinism and power are intimately connected. In
any relationship in which power is unequal (professor
— student; employer — employee; officer — enlisted
personnel; police — suspect) chauvinism is likely to be
going on. John, for example, finds that when he is
acting as a teacher he is inclined to be chauvinistic:
after all, he is the one who has the Ph.D., and he is the
one who has spent all that time preparing a lecture; he
does not take kindly to being challenged by a student.

Jeanne's husband Harney has never been able to
enjoy James Michener's books, because the first one he
read was *Tales of the South Pacific,* which is written
from the point of view of an officer; enlisted men in

general are portrayed as prejudiced, incompetent, and not very bright. Harney spent the same war in the same place, but as a technical sergeant repairing B-29 computers. In his view, officers were those people who interfered with the real work of the base (keeping those bombers flying) by interrupting with silly orders about polishing shoes and keeping your bunk neat.

Chauvinism within a power structure, then, works both ways. The people in power can simplify their thinking by writing off the others as not worth thinking about as individuals, and the people with less power can solidify their ranks by returning the compliment.

Police personnel often stereotype minorities or teenagers; and the minorities and teenagers in turn characterize the police as pigs who are out to get them, with or without cause. Life is simple if you choose up sides once for all and stop thinking. All politicians are crooked . . . never trust anyone over thirty . . . all longhaired boys are drug addicts and probably peddling the stuff, too . . .

Chauvinistic thinking provides a sense of security, it helps remove the ambiguity of life. If you have a blueprint for living, your anxieties are lessened and you feel better. However, chauvinism does not give you the sense of real security which you get when you test your own powers, when you *earn* a sense of being a winner rather than a loser.

Much of chauvinistic thinking is not at all malicious; it is more a matter of thoughtlessness, of assuming that all right-thinking people share your beliefs and your preferences.

One rather trivial example is left-handedness in a right-handed world. About ten or twelve per cent of people are born left-handed. If you are right-handed, you have probably never given a thought to the number of things which have clearly been designed by right-handers for right-handers.

When Jeanne was struggling through penmanship classes in elementary school, parents and teachers alike seemed to believe that being left-handed was a matter of sheer perversity on the part of the child; anybody who really wanted to could learn to be right-handed. Jeanne never did learn to write with her right hand, but she does use scissors and an iron right-handed — because in those days the grips on scissors and the cords on irons were cleverly arranged to make it impossible to use them left-handed.

Now there are several firms at which — for a price — you can find left-handed scissors, can openers, irons, ladles. But you can't find an automobile gearshift, a pay telephone, a door on a public building (except for automatic doors) or a cash register which can be worked equally well with either hand.

This is as it should be. If Jeanne were manufacturing any of these things, she too would design for that 88% of the market rather than for the 12%. On the other hand, have you ever watched a left-handed student trying to cope with taking notes on the right-handed arm of a chair? It takes a good bit of doing, and it certainly does make the student look and feel unduly awkward. This sort of thing has crept into the language: *dextrous* means *right,* while *sinister* and *gauche* mean *left.*

This kind of chauvinism — assuming that the majority is all that matters — is not particularly serious, in this case. Sometimes it has more far-reaching effects.

Let's look at a few of the more common types of chauvinism.

Geography

Nationalism is, of course, a very old form of chauvinism. Loving one's country, respecting its customs, being willing to defend it when necessary, taxing yourself to provide services not just for yourself but for everybody who needs them — all these are admirable attitudes. They may lop over into chauvinism, however, if you feel the need to buttress your country's importance or virtue by scapegoating all other nations, by believing, for example, that the American Way of Life is the ideal for everybody in the world, and that if everybody else just worked a little harder and showed a little more enterprise, they too could have two cars and three television sets and a dishwasher.

We all forget, sometimes, how lucky we in America have been, historically and geographically. We (those of us whose ancestors came from Europe) were provided with an underpopulated continent filled with natural resources so abundant that they seemed for a couple of centuries at least to be inexhaustible.

That is changing now — but don't forget the long head start we had. Our ancestors deserve a lot of credit for their pioneering adventurousness and courage — but the land rewarded them very richly indeed. Some pioneers in other parts of the world had equal degrees of courage and fortitude — they just didn't have our luck. The world is becoming more and more divided into haves and have-nots, country by country and region by region. We must make more of an effort than we have yet to stop thinking chauvinistically and start thinking empathetically about those have-nots.

Geographical chauvinism doesn't necessarily depend on national borders. Have you ever eavesdropped on a conversation between a Texan and an Alaskan?

Or a Los Angeleno and a San Franciscan?

John, when he was sent from Michigan to an army camp in Georgia, discovered that the old story about the child who didn't realize that the phrase "Damn Yankees" was not one word because he had never heard the second half spoken without the first, may well have been true. To the local people, John not only was, but always would be, a "damyankee."

In a state like Colorado, which has most of the industry and most of the population on the eastern side of the Continental Divide, and most of the water on the western side, a legislator from the western slope talking about Denver in the 1980's can sound remarkably like a French diplomat expressing his views on Germany in the 1930's.

Religion

Organized religion lends itself beautifully to chauvinism.

Most religions define themselves by their beliefs, and most religions assume that their beliefs constitute The Truth. If you have The Truth, then everybody who does not share your beliefs must be mistaken.

If you have undergone a personal religious experience — whether it be a mystical experience or a conversion from one faith to another — it's hard to keep your excitement to yourself or to your own inner circle. Your natural (and kindly) impulse is to get out there and tell everybody how great you feel, and how, if they will just accept your belief, they too will feel reborn. You may well be doing the world a service. We can use more enthusiasts.

Just watch out for the equally natural impulse which is likely to follow: your feeling that those who do not accept your particular brand of salvation are either being unduly stubborn or even, perhaps, are downright evil. Carry that to its logical extreme and you eventually get to the attitude of the Catholic Church during the Spanish Inquisition or the Protestant Church under John Calvin: in both cases, the authorities proposed that those who did not share the authorized beliefs were heretics, and that heretics should be dead. And then they saw to it that the heretics became dead.

Christianity is not intrinsically more chauvinistic than other religions. However, in this country, Christians form such an enormous proportion of the population that it is particularly hard for them *not* to be chauvinistic.

The discussion on a recent television talk show centered around a Massachusetts law providing for voluntary prayer in public schools. Any child who wanted to lead the class in prayer might do so; any child who did not want to participate would be allowed to leave the room.

At first blush, this seems innocuous: who could be opposed to letting little kids pray in school if they want to? But think about it a little. Little kids are in general pretty conventional; they do not want to make themselves conspicious in school or appear to be too different from the rest of their classmates. A Jewish or Moslem child might be made very uncomfortable by a Christian prayer; an agnostic child might be made uncomfortable by any prayer at all — yet they would feel even more uncomfortable asking to leave the room during the time set aside for prayer.

During the talk show, somebody called in and stated flatly — perhaps belligerently would be a better word — that anyone who was not a born-again Christian must therefore be a godless Communist and should not be permitted to live in this country, much less express his or her views on religion, or, for that matter, on anything else.

That is religious chauvinism!

Ageism

Those of us in our more or less middle years — say from about 25 to about 60 — tend to be chauvinistic about two groups: the very young and the very old.

Part of this feeling has to do with economics. People are usually reasonably cheerful, or at least resigned, about paying school taxes while their own children are being educated. When those offspring are grown and gone, however, those same people are likely to be much less willing to pay for the education of someone else's kids.

Economics enters into some of the feelings that the middle-aged have about the elderly, too. Every dollar that gets paid out by Social Security or a pension plan is a dollar that gets paid in by someone with a job. If it's your own parent, that's one thing — but you may tend to lump most other older people together and think of them as a group who form a burden for productive taxpayers.

Part of the chauvinistic feeling has to do with power. Children have not yet arrived at power (how long is it since you had to raise your hand if you needed to go to the bathroom?). The elderly, on the other hand, have passed the peak of their power. They may be wiser than they were when they were younger, but if they are retired, they generally don't have the clout that they used to have.

And chauvinism, first and foremost, has to do with power.

Ageism extends to housing patterns: most people who have finished raising their own children are thoroughly tired of raising children; for them, a desirable neighborhood is one which has, at most, a modicum of kids littering the sidewalks with skateboards and tricycles and enlivening the summer air with shrieks of joy or rage.

This makes a certain amount of sense, perhaps; people do tend to value peace and quiet more if they are old enough to have grown children.

Opposition to having older people in the neighborhood doesn't seem so rational — surely the senior citizens are not likely to be wheeling around on unmuffled motorcycles or picking one's petunias without permission. But just try to set up an apartment house or a group home for the elderly in any nice middle class area and see how many people turn up at the zoning hearing, protesting about the "lowering of property values."

Ageism, at both ends of the scale, seems endemic in our society. Maybe we should tell ourselves about once a week at least, that (1) once we were children ourselves; and (2) in a few years more, we ourselves will either be old — or dead.

Racism and Ethnicism

While the most obvious form of racial division is black/white, racism is far from stopping there.

In Minnesota, the 'others' tend to be Indians (as the dominant white group calls them) or Native Americans, as they call themselves. Any good Minnesota chauvinist can tell you that Indians are undependable, casual about time, and inclined to get drunk whenever they can afford to do so.

In the Southwest, the 'others' speak Spanish at home, refuse to buckle down and learn English, have too many children, and don't keep the grass cut.

In California, the Orientals, while hard-working, are clannish and secretive and inscrutable, which makes it hard to trust them.

Jeanne grew up in Chicago, where things are even further refined: everybody in Chicago, even those who have lived there for three or four generations, tends to be a hyphenated American. Politicians look for the Irish vote, the Polish vote, the Italian vote, as well as the black vote and the Puerto Rican vote. People of similar ethnic background are likely to cluster in ethnically pure neighborhoods, and encourage their sons to marry the girl next door. Woe betide the Polish boy who wants to marry a German girl. Both families are going to go right through the ceiling. A melting pot Chicago is not.

Ethnic stereotypes, like other forms of chauvinism, simplify your life; there are whole groups you don't have to think about. Of course, this also means that there are whole groups you will never really know anything about — but if you are a true chauvinist, you know already that they aren't worth exploring.

Sexism

One would think, from the discussions of the past couple of decades, that sexism was a one-way street: men putting down women. In many ways, this picture is not unfair, since men in general have in the past had most of the power, most of the prestige, and most of the money (they still do, but this is changing).

However, women can be sexist, too. Few women have been in a position to turn a man down for employment because "Men are just no good at this kind of job;" on the other hand, it's a rare woman who has never found herself saying, "Everybody knows men are all thumbs when it comes to . . ."

Jeanne discovered a sexist bias in herself. For several years, she was on the speakers' bureau for the League of Women Voters, and every two years she found herself working the men's service club circuit to explain whatever amendments to Colorado law were going to be on the ballot that fall. (One memorable day she had breakfast with the Optimists, lunch with Kiwanis, and dinner with the Lions).

Now LWV is a serious, hard-working, and very efficient organization, and the men's groups formed a sad contrast; since October is not only leading up to Election Day but right in the middle of football season, conversation during the meal centered on what the Denver Broncos had done the previous week and what they were going to do the following week, and Jeanne's introduction as the speaker was almost a formula: "Well, I don't know how much Mrs. Peterson knows about the amendments — although we all admire the great work the League does, don't we, fellows? — but I must say she's easier to look at than most of our speakers. Did I tell you, Mrs. Peterson, that you are the only lady speaker we have ever had?"

Eventually, it dawned on Jeanne (after a lot of soul-searching: did only fatuous men join service clubs?) that she was making an unfair comparison. These clubs all raised money for good causes, all had a serious purpose — but they were also an outlet for all-male conviviality. These men, given a board room or a drafting table, were no doubt competent and efficient; and this is where they worked in the serious way that women worked in LWV.

John had a client who had asked her family doctor to hypnotize her to help her stop smoking. The family doctor failed and referred her to John. It turned out that the client had a few other hang-ups; she was afraid of flying, and if she was in a car she had to be the driver, while her husband was the passenger; his driving made her unbearably nervous.

They had several sessions, and pretty soon John recognized a pattern: the client would ask him for advice but then sabotage it, and report back to him that it hadn't worked. After a little of this, it occurred to John that the solution was simple: this woman simply could not trust a man — any man. She was afraid to fly because most commercial airline pilots are male; she couldn't trust her husband (who was really a capable driver) because he was male; and she couldn't trust John, of course, for the same reason. He sent her to a woman therapist, and at last resort, things were going along very well. That client was a chauvinette.

While we're talking about sexism, we must mention one very important aspect: the attitude of many heterosexual people toward homosexuals. It seems likely that sexual preference, like left-handedness, is either present at birth or caused so soon thereafter that for all practical purposes, the person involved has no real choice. There are about as many homosexuals in our population as there are left-handers; but whereas left-handed people are inconvenienced by the dextrous majority, homosexuals can have their lives shattered by the heterosexual majority.

If you are one of the many who writes off all homosexuals as either perverse or laughable — please think again. Try to feel what it would be like if the situation were reversed — if you were made to feel shame and despair because you were attracted to the opposite sex, when all about you knew that the right, honorable, normal way was to fall in love with someone of your own sex. If you had been a pupil of Plato's — that's the way it would have been.

So — we are all chauvinistic in some respects and to some extent.

Chauvinism is the inverse of intimacy; you can

never become intimate with a member of a group you despise or discount. You are doing yourself — as well as the other group — a disservice by cutting off your options.

To the extent that you are chauvinistic, you are not appreciating the human condition, and you are therefore missing a lot of life.

We all have much more in common than we have in the way of dissimilarities. Appreciate the differences — and be human with the other humans on this earth.

*How Do You Know
You've Arrived?*

How Do You Know
You've Arrived?
(Success)

What does success mean to you? Money? Fame? Career advancement? A happy private life? A good sense of selfworth? The definitions of success are as enormously varied as the human beings on the earth. And "success," in this broad sense of "Now, there goes a successful man," applies *only* to human beings.

Think about elephants, for example. A member of an elephant herd is a successful elephant, whether or not she is the leader. (Did you know that leaders of elephant herds are always females, usually older and presumably wiser?) The mature male elephants who are driven out of the group may be taken on by another group of females who need breeding partners, or they may lead lonely lives out there in the jungle. However, even those isolated male elephants are still elephants; doesn't the phrase, "Now, there goes a successful elephant," sound a bit peculiar?

Elephants, apes, wolves vary in dexterity, hunting skills, size, age, sex — they are successful on one forage for food and unsuccessful on another; successful in defeating another male and establishing a harem on one occasion, unsuccessful on another. So far as anybody has been able to ascertain, a wolf does not go around saying to itself, "Damn! I missed that caribou. I'm a real failure as a wolf."

We, on the other hand, are brought up from infancy to think in terms of success and failure, and we have a strong tendency to internalize and extrapolate those terms: "I didn't pass the math test," is often converted into, "I never will be any good at math," and thence into, "I'm stupid at math; I'm a failure."

The better you are at avoiding extrapolations like that, the better your life is likely to be. However, you will reach a point — when you have a serious illness from which you think you might not recover, for example — when you will find yourself spending a period of time contemplating your past life and deciding how well you have spent your time; whether your life *as a whole* has been a success. When that time comes, will you feel successful, or will you be overcome by despair at the memory of the opportunities you missed, the relationships you didn't have, the times you failed?

How do you achieve the happy feeling of fulfillment, of having arrived where you want to be? You begin at the beginning if you can; otherwise, you start from where you are.

Back to the basics

You spend your very first years of life just getting acquainted with your world. By the time you are in third or fourth grade, you are able to start dealing with abstract concepts. That is, you can consider a problem which says, "If it takes two men twelve hours to lay a brick wall measuring . . ." without needing to see the men or the bricks, or to spend the stated twelve hours watching them build that wall. You can also work with mental imagery. "What would happen if I just didn't go to school tomorrow, if I went fishing instead? Mom might call the school (but she doesn't do that very often), somebody might see me going in the wrong direction, the school bus driver might notice I'm not on the bus and call my house, the teacher might say something to the principal . . . maybe I'd better go to school."

By the time you are a young adolescent (and nowadays, this can be as young as ten or eleven), you begin to look at possibilities; your emphasis shifts from the real to the possible. You test out various roles, you try to validate your ideas experimentally. "There's that girl who doesn't like me very much; maybe I'll try telling her I really like the way she fixes her hair. Or I could ask her if she would like to come over and do homework together tonight; I'm better at history than she is . . ." "I think I'm pretty good at gymnastics; maybe I should sign up for the talent show and see whether other people think so too."

You are, as an adolescent, future-oriented ("When I grow up . . . when I get out of high school . . . I'm never going to . . .")

You begin to play different roles, to see where your particular, unique talents lie. Too often, this process is random, unplanned, and very chancy.

If you are an adolescent, see if your school offers aptitude and interest tests; you may be surprised at some of the things they can turn up about your hidden talents and interests. If you are the parents of an adolescent, look into testing; you owe it to the kid. And you will both be much happier if your child learns at an early age what would be the most productive paths to follow. Following along after one's real, though perhaps unknown, interests and aptitudes adds a special third dimension to life.

Don't decide too early — or let your child decide too early — what he or she is going to be "when you grow up." Adolescents generally have a pretty shaky sense of identity, and may lock into something unsuitable just so they can say to themselves, their parents, their friends, "What I am is the leader of a rock band . . ." "expecting a baby . . ." "the prettiest cheerleader this school ever had . . ." Temporary identities are all right, as long as they don't cut off future options, as long as they aren't a case of premature closure.

John and his brothers played in a jazz band during high school, and for a time talked about becoming professional musicians. They still enjoy playing together, but they all chose different careers. Not that there is anything wrong with being a professional musician, jazz or otherwise, of course: the important thing is that you should give yourself time to explore various options.

People sometimes feel that by the time they are eighteen or twenty years old, they should have their lives mapped out. Not so. You may be a late bloomer, so to speak; five or more years slower than your contemporaries in finding your true vocation. Jeanne's daughter Susan, for example, had a socially stimulating but academically mediocre career in high school. Then she spent a year at jobs which took good looks, a pleasant personality, manual dexterity, or some combination of these: she was a model, a waitress, a restaurant hostess, a door to door saleswoman, a nurses' aide; and decided that none of these looked like a satisfactory permanent career for her. She took a twelve-month course and emerged as a licensed practical nurse, worked at this for a year or two, decided that she loved the work but wanted more theory, and went to college. She had a couple of years of pre-nursing courses, switched to pre-medical courses, and in her senior year finally decided that she would rather be a veterinarian than a "people" doctor. All of this has been a little disconcerting to parents who were brought up to believe that you got to stop paying tuition when your youngest child was twenty-one or so, but at the same time it has been deeply rewarding to watch her enthusiasm and her academic achievements increase as she gradually zeroed in to what she wants to be "when she grows up."

In contrast, there is one of John's clients, a talented artist who didn't realize that monetary rewards for artistic achievement do not usually come early or in large amounts. At the age of 24, he decided to become an accountant, just because he knew he could make money at it. Security just should not be that important at that age. If you don't like what you are doing, by all means change; if you do like what you are doing, hang in there for awhile and have faith that eventually somebody else will like what you are doing well enough to pay you for it.

If you do not like what you are doing, even if you are middle-aged, see if you can change careers. Some people can easily afford to do this. A couple of John's clients, for instance, are both lawyers. The husband gave up his practice and is spending a year building a house, supported by the wife, who is still a practicing lawyer. Financially, this couple can afford the risk; psychologically, the husband is taking a bigger chance. Every time you change your career, you lose part of your sense of identity. You find yourself with a new set of problems, having to perfect a new set of skills. Suppose that lawyer turns out to be no great shakes at building a house? Well, he can always go back to practicing law.

Meanwhile, he will have learned some things about himself. You must be willing to take risks, both economic risks and risks with your own sense of self-worth, in order to give yourself a chance at success. If you do not achieve the success you hoped for (earn that

million dollars, get that patent, build that ideal house),
you still have not failed; you know yourself better now
than you did before you tried, and that in itself is a form
of success.

As we were saying back there, what is success?

Money

Too many people equate success with money. This is
a primitive way of thinking. Money is nice to have, but
it is, after all, a tool and only a tool. You use it to get
what you want. You may be satisfied with enough
money to keep the children fed and clothed and the
utility bill paid; you may want to have so much that
you never have to ask the price of anything; you may
hope for a secure retirement; you may want to travel.
The money in itself is just a means to your end.

The process by which you get money may be
important to your feeling of success. If you buy a stock
just before it doubles in value, you can congratulate
yourself on your astute reading of the market, or on
your skill in picking the broker who got you to invest in
that particular stock. That's what enhances your
feeling of self-worth; the money is just a symbol.

Our society is so accustomed to identifying money
with success that it is very difficult for a low income
person to feel a good sense of self-worth. Stop and think
about our society's values for a moment. Given a
choice, would you rather be deprived for two months of
your favorite television sitcom, or of your trash
collection? When your expected baby turns out to be
triplets, would you rather have the presence of that
rock group which is pulling in the crowds downtown, or
of one competent nurse's aide? Yet when is the last time
you asked your trashman (or telephone repairman, or
police agent, or snowplow operator) for his or her
autograph?

The world's most underrated occupation

This — society's tendency to equate money with success — is one of the reasons that fulltime wives and mothers find it difficult, sometimes, to feel a good sense of selfworth. The trash collector at least gets his salary counted by the government in figuring up the Gross National Product each year. None of a homemaker's contributions — none of the cooking, cleaning, childraising, chauffeuring, counselling — get counted, unless she does them in somebody else's household, for money.

Elaine Morgan, in *The Descent of Woman,* puts it well: "It is possible, as we know, to have too many people, just as we may have overproduction of any other commodity like potatoes or fish — and it has even more disastrous results because it is harder to plow them back in or throw them back into the sea — but every society recognizes in a thousand ways that the one thing it can't altogether dispense with is people, properly processed competent people to take their turn at operating all the intricate processes of production and administration when the present operators get past it."

The trouble is that, in spite of all the lipservice our society gives to the importance of the family, in spite of Mother's Day and the Year of the Child, it doesn't act as if it thinks these things are important. And if nobody else seems to think what you are doing is important, it takes enormous strength of character to stay convinced that your priorities are the right ones for you, that you did make the right choices, that success, for you at least, is not going to be measured in terms of money.

What are the terms in which you are going to measure it, then? You are trying to give your husband emotional support, and to meet your children's emotional needs. Homemaking involves a lot of physical effort, but even more psychic effort; you are likely to spend a fair amount of time wondering just where lies the balance between overprotectiveness and child neglect, between pampering and pushing; between overinquisitiveness and indifference.

One clear criterion of success for you is how are the kids turning out? It's a dangerous one, though; because no matter how good a mother you are, how consistent, how hard you try — nobody can guarantee that your kids, any more than any other human beings, are going to be just what you had hoped they would.

You must just do the best you can — and sustain your own sense of self worth by knowing that you did do the best you could — no matter how you feel about the product at any given moment.

Fame, to some people, means success. Do you want to be so well-known that you can get the best table in any restaurant you happen to drop into? To win a Nobel prize? To have two out of every three people you meet on the street ask you for your autograph?

Ask yourself whether you really want that level of fame. The track record of movie stars, adulated singers, and even literary geniuses gives one pause: all that alcohol, all those drugs, all those hospitalizations for stress or nervous exhaustion.

You may be happier if you settle for a more modest sort of fame — as the lady who has manned the volunteer desk at the hospital every Thursday for ten years, including the Thursday on which she went into labor with her third child; the man who always offers to follow up on the pledge cards that somebody missed during the fund drive; the friend who can always be counted on to provide a meal, a bed, or a shoulder suitable for weeping on.

Career advancement is another handy way to measure success. But what do you mean by success? Or advancement? In the business world, as in academia, advancement often means stopping doing what you do best, and like best, to go into administration. If you are a good teacher, you are going to become chairman of the department, and have less time left for teaching. If you are a very good teacher, you may become principal, or dean, or president, or headmaster, and have no time at all left for teaching.

If you are a good salesman, you are likely to become head of the sales department, where you may be valuable explaining to other people how you achieved your rapport with the customers, but you won't have the thing itself — the pleasure of closing a difficult deal — any more. If you are a good chemist, you get to be in charge of the laboratory and spend most of your time hiring, firing, and allocating the time of other people, while your own research sits there neglected.

And career advancement, as measured by somebody else's criteria, doesn't mean much if you don't want to do what you are doing. John has another couple as clients: the husband is a "successful" physician, and the wife is a nurse. They both took aptitude and interest tests, and the husband now feels that his real vocation is that of engineering. He may or may not go back and start over; he has a lot of time, money and effort invested in his present career. The wife, who became a nurse when any nice middle class girl trained to become a teacher, a secretary, or a nurse while waiting for the right man to turn up, has no doubts. She scored very high in structural visualization, and she is going to go back to school with the intention of becoming an architect.

Now, these people can afford to play around with second chances on careers. What if you can't? If you have a job, rather than a career, and you don't see any way out of it, you may have to get your satisfactions outside of working hours.

Jeanne's husband Harney is a remarkably versatile man. He is a chemist, and when for a time he headed the laboratory, he absolutely hated it; he agonized every time he had to let somebody go, he loathed making up work schedules and supervising other people's work. After a fairly brief interlude, he asked the company to find somebody else and let him go back to research. This, as anybody knows, is *not* the way up the corporate ladder; he never got to be a vice president, and he never will.

However, for seventeen years he did a radio show on traditional jazz, a field in which he is an authority. He and Jeanne built their own house. He has a small glassblowing business which will become larger when he retires from the large company he still works for. Recently, he rigged up a solar water heater for the house, and the current project is a solar greenhouse.

Harney, in other words, is expressing his interests and expertise in two areas: within the corporate structure by being a chemist; outside it for his other varied activities.

We like John's father's definition of success: "Set out on a project and make it work." You have to pick your project — John admires Harney's greenhouse, but it would be the last thing in the world he would try to do himself. He once put together a prefabricated doghouse in his basement, ignoring his son's warnings that it would never go through the door. Sure enough, it didn't go through the door. He had to take it apart and start all over again. On the other hand, Harney can't play drums (although he can play a mean washboard). Because of the way they feel about themselves, because of their willingness to risk failure on the chance of success, because of their unwillingness to stake their whole feeling of self worth on any one definition — psychologist, chemist, drummer, housebuilder, inventor, or any other one thing — they are both successful men. Successful men who have had the occasional failure. As do we all.

Success, in other words, is not tied in irrevocably with money, fame, career advancement — unless that is your own private definition.

Success means doing what you can to fulfill your own private dreams. More than one of John's clients, then asked about their private fantasy, will say, "I don't like even to think about it; I'm afraid I'll be disappointed." Go ahead, think about it; what can you lose? And then if you possibly can, do something about it.

What if you don't have any private dreams? You just haven't contemplated your own soul thoroughly enough. Think if you were to die tomorrow, what would you regret? What would you like to have accomplished? How close are you? It isn't a matter of how many projects you have carried out; it's a matter of the risks you took, the time you spent, the quality of effort, the commitment you made in psychic energy, to something that has been important to you.

Above all else, it involves being true to yourself.

One of John's clients has given us permission to use some information about her father.

He came from a large family with a tradition of never offering, asking for, or accepting help — emotional or financial — from each other. As the children grew up, they scattered to various parts of the country and kept in only very loose touch with each other. He worked his way through college, married when he was 22, and lost his first job (this was in the depths of the Depression) almost immediately. A long series of career changes followed. Although all his jobs took intelligence, writing talent, and organizational ability, all of which he had in abundance, none of them paid well enough to satisfy either his own parents or his wife's parents.

From his daughter's point of view, he was not an ideal parent. Although she remembers a number of happy occasions, she also remembers him as very authoritarian, a strict disciplinarian, who would never permit his children to contradict him or to express anger, and would never talk about interpersonal relationships.

From his wife's point of view, he was not an ideal husband. Although he was supportive and encouraging in some ways, he would never permit her to have any life apart from him. She was talented, creative, and a born teacher, and would have liked to work outside the home, but he would not allow this.

John's client says: "He had hundreds of friends all of whom respected him for his dedication, honesty, reliability and education and talents . . . My mother felt she was a failure in every way and my father believed he was a great success in that he had maintained his good reputation for honesty and integrity throughout his life. He never admitted to any faults or blame."

He had many friends, but he had no intimates; his daughter says, "He said that I was the only one he could talk to and we seldom got to really intimate things. When we did, I often disagreed and when that happened, he would just get quiet and not respond or leave and go to another room or to bed. This is what he would do whenever there was unpleasantness or anything he thought disagreeable. . .just withdraw."

In spite of having spent a lifetime without emotional intimacy, this man died feeling successful — because to him honesty and integrity were all-important, and he had lived up to his own ideals in this respect.

This man was not a perfect husband, a perfect father, or an outstanding breadwinner. He was not even what you might call a well-rounded personality. He was — like all the rest of us — a fallible human being. But he died happy because he had been true to himself.

"Integrity" is often equated with "honesty;" but its first meaning is "wholeness." If you act with consistency, if you maintain your integrity throughout your life, you, too, can die happy. We all will die; dying happy is an important part of life.

It's Not What You Do,
It's the Way That You Do It

It's Not What You Do,
It's the Way That You Do It
(Coping with Stress)

Sandra Smith, M.D., has a busy obstetrical practice. As she drives to the hospital on this cold November morning, she reflects with pleasure on the fact that her day off — tomorrow — coincides with her 45th birthday. She and Jim can have dinner at the country club, and her answering service will direct her calls to her partner. Sixteen years ago, she remembers, she was in her last year of residency at this very hospital. Thirty-six hours on, and twelve hours off. Would she *ever* catch up on her sleep? Still, it was good training for an obstetrician; babies still had a way of arriving at inconvenient times, and her ability to snatch a few hours of sleep whenever possible was still very useful indeed.

Central Hospital, she thinks, as she slides the Mercedes into her reserved spot, has more than doubled in size since her days as a resident. Well, so has the town. Even with the passing of the "baby boom," she still has more than enough to do. This morning, for instance, two Caesarian sections, and Mrs. — what *is* the woman's name? — Mrs. Ferguson was just about due. Then there's the staff meeting this afternoon, and office hours after that. Maybe she should consider taking on another partner; she isn't as young as she used to be. Still, she has never regretted her choice; obstetrics is not the easiest specialty, but she thinks it is one of the most rewarding ones. How long since she's had a real vacation, more than a long weekend? If Jim can arrange things with his law partners, maybe they could go to Bermuda — or Martinique — or New Zealand. It would be spring now in New Zealand; she is tired of winter already, and here it is only November. Perhaps she really does need a vacation; she must give that some thought.

Julie Jones, L.P.N., is also on her way to the hospital. As she waits, transfer in hand, for the bus that will take her within a couple of blocks of Central Hospital, she notices that the rain is beginning to turn to sleet. It will probably be snowing hard by the time her shift is over. That means the buses will be running late, and she won't have time to stop at the corner grocery before the kids get home from school. What does she have in the pantry? Tuna, mushroom soup, noodles, potato chips, canned pears — yes, that will do for tonight's dinner; if the weather gets better, she'll do her shopping tomorrow instead.

She wonders whether her daughter Nancy is getting too involved with that Kerrigan boy. Now that the high school is on double shifts, the kids have entirely too much free time. Nancy is nearly seventeen. Ah, well, when Julie herself was seventeen, she was already going steady with Len. A good man, on the whole, Len, although he never would make much money. And inclined to take a drop too much now and then. Still, a good husband and a good father; a hard worker.

As the second bus drops her at the corner nearest the hospital, she reflects that Central certainly has grown since she got her training as a licensed practical nurse here all those years ago. Let's see, she'd been nineteen then, and now she was almost forty-five. Worked on and off — between babies — ever since. The work has changed over the years; she is now doing the sort of patient care that the registered nurses used to do when she was a beginner; the aides are doing what she used to do; the registered nurses are mostly supervising, except for giving I.V.'s. She can't give I.V.'s but she does give medications, change dressings, take blood pressure readings . . . and it seems like every time she comes to work there are more patients squeezed into her ward. Well, it's a job, and she ought to be grateful to have it, she supposes.

Which of these women is more likely to develop high blood pressure, or an ulcer, or chronic headaches?

Contrary to conventional wisdom, the busy physician, to whom life and death decisions are a commonplace, whose sleep is interrupted by emergencies, who works long and sometimes erratic hours, who is responsible for training and supervising other people — is in a much less stressful position than is the nurse.

Sandra Smith likes her job. She chose it because she thought it would be interesting and rewarding, and it is. She gets high returns — in prestige and in money — and, most important of all, she gets a high degree of control of her life. Sure, she reponds to midnight calls. But she has a partner, and could have more than one, to whom she could delegate the night calls should she want to. She has enough money to take short breaks or long vacations whenever she wants to do so, and enough money to spend her free time being anywhere in the world, doing anything she has a mind to do.

Julie Jones works because she has to. She does her eight hours at the hospital with a divided mind, with an ever-increasing sense of pressure. She has more patients than she used to have, and she is expected to do more things for and to them than her early training had led her to expect. She has no control over her environment at the hospital, and not much more control over her environment at home. She gets satisfactions from her husband and her children; she also worries about them. They expect her (and she expects herself) to see that dinner is ready, the laundry is done, the living room is dusted, the younger children get help with their homework, the older ones don't take to stealing hubcaps or getting pregnant in a casual affair — all in her spare time.

Sandra Smith has a lot of responsibility. She also has a lot of control. When she is doing her two Caesarian sections this morning, the rest of the operating team is going to do precisely what she tells them to do.

Julie Jones also has a lot of responsibility. She is a nurse, a wife, and a mother. But she has very little control over her life. As a nurse, she follows orders from registered nurses, supervisors, and physicians. As a wife, she defers to her husband. As a mother, she does what she can for her children, and worries that she isn't doing enough.

As to whether either of them will develop a stress-related disease, nobody can say for certain. It depends not only on the amount of stress to which each is subjected, but how long the stress goes on, and most important of all, how she reacts to it. Some people have equable, placid temperaments and react to stress with less anxiety than would seem possible to anybody looking at their situation from outside. Other people fly apart at what an onlooker would suppose to be rather trivial stresses.

We tend to think of stress in very negative terms: stress is pressure, something unpleasant, anxiety-producing, like getting arrested, getting fired, getting divorced, getting pregnant when you don't want to.

This is not necessarily so.

172

The human body is a remarkably conservative organism. It reacts to *any* change in its usual environment as stress. (This may well come from the days when surprises were much more likely to be unpleasant — cave bears, sabre-toothed tigers — than pleasant — the first ripe berry, the unexpected antelope).

In any case, it was much more important for the survival of the species that human beings reacted to new situations with doubt, suspicion, and a readiness to run, than that they embraced all new experiences with interest, joy, and curiosity. Both of those reactions operated then, and they operate now; but the first was more important. We wouldn't be here at all if our ancestors had been conditioned to try to make friends with large, hungry carnivores.

According to Dr. Hans Selye, who is the acknowledged expert in this field, "Stress is the response of the body to any demand placed upon it." Whether you get married or divorced, promoted or fired, your body is going to perceive the change as stressful. First it will go into an alarm reaction to fight the demand; hormones are released that stimulate the heartbeat and respiration rate and cause muscles to tense. (Next time you're making love, think about that; isn't what you're feeling a stress reaction?) Next, your body will adapt to the demand. That sounds good, and it is; the only catch is that if you *over*adapt to continued stress, you may get such unpleasant effects as a heart attack, arthritis, an ulcer, high blood pressure, and/or an attack of the common cold. Finally, if the stress is great enough or prolonged enough, you get exhaustion. If you're tough or lucky, you recover from the exhaustion or the stress lessens; if you're more sensitive or unlucky, the stress continues or intensifies, you become less able to cope with it, and you wind up with one of the stress-related diseases, or with some form of mental illness. If the stress can be reduced, you will probably get better. John once had a rather disconcerting encounter with a white-coated person in a mental hospital who was supervising the lunchroom. He turned out to be, not a member of the staff, as John had initially assumed, but a patient. In the protective environment of the hospital, separated from the stress that had caused his illness, he was operating in a perfectly normal way.

The well-known Social Readjustment Rating Scale developed by Drs. Holmes, Holmes, Rahe and Arthur over the last decade or so is revealing. On a scale working down from 100, death of your spouse, as you might expect, is 100, while divorce is 73. (Jeanne is somewhat skeptical about this; surely it would depend upon the circumstances of the spouse's demise or departure). Anyway, the first six items are all clearly negative events. But seventh (tucked in between "personal injury or illness" and "fired at work" comes "marriage." Ninth is "marital reconciliation." Eighteenth is "business readjustment." It doesn't seem to matter whether the adjustment is upward or downward; your body perceives the change as stressful. Even an "outstanding personal achievement" gives you 28 stress points, while a vacation gives you 13, Christmas deals you out 12, and a minor violation of the law only turns up 11. The point of the scale is that if you come up with 300 or above on the total scale, your risk of developing a major illness within the next two years is — about 80%. Your body, which apparently still thinks it is living among the Neanderthals, is likely to do you in. And if your body doesn't get you, your mind well may.

How to cope? Some of the currently popular self-help

books suggest that you reject the demands of other people, thus reducing your own stress. We would prefer a compromise: realize that you do, unless you are a lifelong hermit, have obligations to at least a few other people, if not to society as a whole, but consider your life situation and see whether you can reduce the stress in your life or alter your response to that stress — or maybe both.

One of John's clients came to him, referred by his physician, because his arthritis had become so crippling that he could no longer hold a tennis racket, and tennis (along with jogging, golf, handball, and sundry other similar activities) was very important to him. The client was 35 years old, and in what almost anybody would consider a high-stress job: he was an air traffic controller. It took only a session or two for John to realize that his client was intelligent, knowledgeable in a number of different fields — and neither expressive nor assertive. He would ask questions, but be unable to express his own feelings. His wife was rigid, opinionated, and clearly in control of the family. She prided herself on being willing to give somebody a piece of her mind. He maintained a very low profile, but seemed pleased when his wife would express his hostility for him. On the other hand, he clearly felt somewhat hostile to her now and then, but couldn't express how he felt.

Once he managed to get in touch with his own feelings of anger, and learned how to express them himself, without depending on his wife to do the job for him — his arthritis gave up. It didn't disappear completely, but it got so much better that he is now back being his old athletic self.

This man had a combination of a high-stress job and an inability to express his feelings about the job or about any other area of his life. What he needed was therapy to help him become more expressive and more assertive.

Another of John's clients had a different, but still stress-related, problem. He was 28 years old, an engineering technician, and was going to school part-time to get his engineering degree. Meanwhile, he worked for a small, very promising company. He was the trouble-shooter; his office was at the back of a long hallway, and it often used to take him 45 minutes to make it to his office in the morning; people kept popping out of doorways to ask him what to do about their current crisis. There always were crises; he spent his time, so to speak, putting out brushfires instead of being able to get on with his own work. Added to this stress was his concern about his own future with the company. He felt the company had enormous potential and he would like to grow with it, but top management had gone through two major reorganizations in the last couple of years, and he worried whether the next reorganization would reach down into his own middle management echelon.

He came to John because of constant headaches. Friday evenings, he mentioned, he used to relax by drinking eight or nine shots of bourbon and smoking a joint or two. He realized this was a bit excessive, but he needed the relaxation; however, between his recreational weekends and his constant severe headaches, his grades were beginning to slip, he thought his job might be in jeopardy, and he was, all in all, pretty miserable.

John suggested that he should keep a diary and write down the times when he felt particularly pressured. After a few weeks of that, it became crystal clear to him that it was his job that was the problem. He quit. The headaches stopped instantly. The bourbon and the pot stopped being essential relaxants. He got a lower-pressure job with a big, established company. He is working as an engineering technician, and going on to complete his engineering degree (the new company is paying his tuition) and he can get his job done between nine and five. He has time to recharge his psychic batteries, to reflect on what he's going to do tomorrow — what he's going to want to be doing five years from now. He has a great need to achieve and accomplish things; he won't be happy in a low pressure job for long. But right now, it's exactly what he needs — a brief respite from stress.

How can you, yourself, cope with stress?

We go back once again to one of our favorite phrases: "The unexamined life is not worth living." To put it another way, first you decide whether you are more a Type A or a Type B person. This is a somewhat oversimplified division of people according to general temperament. Type A people are competitive, impatient, and have a very high drive toward achievement. These are the people who, when everything else is equal, are going to have more than their share of ulcers, heart attacks, strokes, and other undesirable physical ailments. Type B people are basically considerably more relaxed, and tend to muddle through somehow without major mental or physical impairment.

However, even Type B people can find themselves in situations where relaxation doesn't seem to be an adequate response. Jeanne remembers one horrible year when she decided to drop all her desultory volunteer activities — a League of Women Voters committee here, an ACLU committee there, a church skit, a hospital fund raising letter — and take a paying job at the local junior high school, running a resource center. This consisted of showing the bright kids, who were on independent study programs, where they could find the right resource materials, helping the slow kids, who tended to be funneled out to the resource center because they were disruptive in the classrooms, to comprehend seventh grade geography or eighth grade math or whatever, grading papers, working up sociograms (a sociogram is a sort of rough chart showing who likes whom and who hates whom) of the participants in the Trojan War, and listening sympathetically to kids whose parents had too little money, too much money, too little time, too much time . . . Well, it was an interesting job. And two of her three kids were students there.

Meanwhile, Susie, the oldest, got a case of mononucleosis so severe that she would fall asleep in the middle of a sentence. Jeanne arranged for a homebound teacher.

Alan, the youngest, broke his leg, and it turned out that the leg broke because he had a bone cyst, and they tried a bone graft, and the bone graft got infected, and Alan, who was 12 and had the usual growing boy's appetite, got so tired of being hospitalized (three months, altogether) that he refused to eat, and Jeanne was grading finals at his bedside, and meanwhile Susie, who was recovering from her mononucleosis and feeling like socializing again, was running a surreptitious crash pad from her bedroom, and Harney, who had up until then enjoyed a reasonably satisfactory life as a research chemist, was suddenly burdened with a supervisor who was a manager rather than a scientist, and who would say things like, "Now we need results on this by Friday."

Well, the whole family was severely stressed.

Everybody reacted differently, and everybody was pretty unhappy, including the middle child, Karen, who had at the moment no personal problems with broken bones, unreasonable employers, mononucleosis, or parental disapproval of one's associates. Everybody recovered, but everybody suffered for awhile.

So much for being a Type B.

If you are a Type A, watch out. Your personality probably is a result of learned behavior, and maybe you can unlearn it. If not, you should think through the stress-producing aspects of your life, and see if you can either reduce some of them, or find better ways of coping with them.

Are you in a dead-end job? Or a job which carries more pressure than you can — or want to — cope with? Can you change the job? Delegate more responsibility? Go to night school and qualify for something you would like better?

Many of us are in positions we can't change — work positions, that is. If we can't get satisfactions from our jobs, we'd better try to get them from our home life, our hobbies, our church, our political activities.

Stress — perceived stress — comes not only from high pressure work but from boredom. (Yes, that does seem peculiar, doesn't it? Maybe that too comes from caveman days, when too many winter days, with no edible herds crossing the horizon, induced a feeling of stress in our ancestors). If your job is boring, can you do something about it? If you can't improve your job, can you improve your extracurricular activities? Take a course, take a lover, take a few minutes to think about yourself?

That, really, is where the answer is: thinking about **yourself. You are unique; your answer to stress will be** unique. John's answer is jogging. He jogs about six miles a day, five days a week. It dissipates his anxieties, and makes him more open to classroom questions, discussion, perhaps disagreement with his views . . . (anxiety producing!)

Jogging may be the answer for you — exercise of some sort is the answer for a lot of people. Better relationships with people you love is the answer for others. More responsibility, less responsibility, more predictability, more excitement, less boredom — the answers are different, because we all differ from each other.

The one constant is a double one.

There are two immutable laws of life: (1) Life is unpredictable. (2) There are no permanent solutions.

This means, does it not, that stress will always be with us? How else could we learn, could we grow, could we change at all?

It isn't stress *per se* which is harmful; it's our reaction to it. If you can manage to reduce your stress to a reasonable level, and if you can change your attitude to stressful events, to think of stress as a challenge rather than a burden — well, that's probably what Mother Nature had in mind in the old cave days, and what is still best for us as individuals and as a species today.

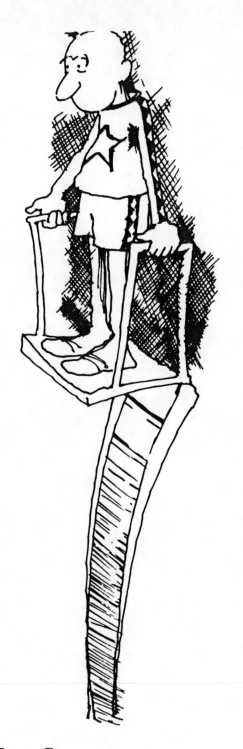

To Be or Not to Be

To Be or Not to Be
(Taking Risks)

Hamlet, of course, was thinking of physical death —
suicide — in that famous "To be or not to be . . ."
soliloquy. But if you opt for perfect security (as if there
were any such thing) rather than risk-taking, you are
lining yourself up for a sort of psychic death.

Security is a basic human need; the human race
would not survive if babies could not count on a certain
amount of security. Babies need first to feel protected,
they need to be warm, fed, cuddled, loved. Only after
that need for basic security is met can they reach out
and begin to become real human beings.

Once infancy is over, people still need a certain
amount of security, but that need is what Adler would
call a lower level need. When that level of needs is
satisfied, people need more — they must take risks. It is
only by taking risks (sensible risks, not ridiculous
ones) that you maintain or enhance your sense of self-
worth. You need to feel that your input in a situation is
important, that your presence makes a difference. You
need a sense of competence, of mastery. You achieve
that feeling only by taking risks. You owe it to yourself
to take some risks — even if you fail. As G. K.
Chesterton put it, "Whatever is worth doing is worth
doing badly."

Whenever you set out to master a new skill, you begin
by doing it badly: you miss the ball, you fall off the
water skis, you can't find the right notes on the piano.

Only practice, time, and determination will improve your performance. Every time you try to enlarge your field of operations, you risk your sense of self-worth; but oddly enough, it is only by taking risks that you can maintain your sense of self-worth. If you choose to be safe, comfortable, and static, pretty soon you won't like yourself as well as you used to.

Human beings need to test themselves, to try new adventures, to achieve a feeling of competence. Only by taking risks do you grow as a human personality.

What do you think of when you consider risk?

Careering around corners on a motorcycle? Tubing down a mountain stream during the spring run-off? Staking your last five dollars on a game in Las Vegas? Leaving your safe job with a large company for one which has a lot more potential — if the new company survives its first few shaky years? Letting another person know of your love, even though you risk rejection?

What people consider risky is very idiosyncratic. It depends not only on individual temperament, but on age.

Physical risks

Children, for instance, have no real sense of mortality. Even adolescents have a feeling of personal invulnerability. Many a teen-aged girl has been astonished to find herself pregnant. That's the sort of thing that's supposed to happen to somebody else, never to you, yourself. And many a teen-aged boy has wound up in the hospital after discovering that trying to take that corner at eighty miles an hour violated one or more laws of physics, as well as the local traffic ordinances.

The young will take physical risks that seem insane to most of their elders. The psychic gains they get from the risk-taking are well worth it to them, as long as their luck holds, and even, sometimes, if it doesn't hold.

John's son Chris is highly competitive; he needs to be fastest, first, best. He's a good skier, but nobody would ever call him a cautious one. His drive to win is far more powerful than any qualms about his own safety.

John skis, too. He used to be a downhill skier until he broke his leg on a slope some years ago. When his kids were beginning to get interested in the sport, he considered taking it up again. Until he heard the instructor say, "You have to *attack* the hill!" John, to whom jogging is a very important part of life, decided that putting himself in an adversary position with a mountain did not make a lot of sense. Bones approaching their fifth decade do not mend as easily as bones in their second decade, and if he broke his leg again, there went the jogging. John settled for cross-country skiing. Chris, of course, never gave a thought to broken bones; something like that couldn't happen to *him!*

Children and adolescents, then, tend to take risks of a physical sort with a blithe indifference to possible consequences.

Emotional risks

Emotional risks are something else again. Adolescents, engaged in building their identities, are painfully susceptible to peer pressure. Being rejected as a person, having the one you love turn you down (for marriage, for an affair, even for a single date) is excruciatingly difficult to cope with.

Think back to your own high school days. Were you ever as afraid of an exam or a volleyball game as you were of going to a party? If you asked someone to go with you, would you be turned down? If you went alone, would anybody talk to you or dance with you? Would you feel stupid, tongue-tied, rejected? The risks involved in a social situation are, for most teen-agers, absolutely enormous.

Adolescents, fortunately, seem to sense that everybody in their age bracket suffers from this problem. That's why there is so much of the best-friend-rumor-spreading: "Carol told me that Linda said that Marsha thinks you're great." This gives the boy concerned a chance to make a tentative advance without risking his whole psyche on a completely unknown quantity, while giving the girl concerned an out if she really isn't crazy about him after one date — or if he never calls her. After all, *she* didn't say — directly to him — "I would like to go out with you."

This business of emotional vulnerability also explains the maddening popularity of telephones among adolescents; expressing your feelings over a telephone wire is far less risky than doing so face to face.

The second time around

Emotional risk-taking is perhaps most difficult for adolescents, but it isn't easy for most adults, either. If, for instance, you have recently been widowed or divorced and are trying the singles scene again, you may feel just the way you did when you were in junior high school: awkward, inept, and far too vulnerable to rejection from somebody else.

In theory, if you are, say, thirty or forty, your sense of self-worth should not be that tied up in rejection or acceptance by somebody of the opposite sex. In practice, unfortunately, if your self-definition is rather shaky, you are likely to regress to adolescence. And death or divorce of a spouse is likely to have that kind of effect, for awhile — your self-definition while your marriage lasted involved, among other things, being part of a married couple. Even if your marriage was one you are relieved to be rid of, it may take you awhile to settle down and be the new you.

If your marriage has ended in divorce, you feel like a failure. Women, especially, have been programmed by our society to believe that most of the responsibility for keeping a marriage going belongs to them. Find out, before you begin looking for a serious relationship, what your own needs are now; they do change over time. And then be up front; if you want to get married again, say so. Begin thinking, "That ex-husband of mine really missed the boat; I'm going to make somebody a *wonderful* wife!"

Meanwhile, remember that it is possible to start building new relationships on your own terms. Say you are a woman: you meet somebody who seems attractive and interested in you (but how good a judge are you, just now, of people?) You don't have to wind up at either his apartment or yours sooner than you want to. You can give him your telephone number but not your address; you can meet over coffee in the afternoon, or lunch in a public place, until you are more sure of your feelings and expectations — and of his.

A great many people feel that there is necessarily going to be a loss of control on their part if a new relationship is going to be meaningful; they are afraid to fall in love because they are afraid the other person will take advantage of them. Well, it may be so; or it may work out well for both people. Keep in mind that you can fall in love without being infatuated; that is, you can be a warm, loving, reasonably trusting person — but nobody says you have to be stupid about it!

You have to decide what you really want, and then you have to decide what risks you are willing to take to achieve your goals. Consider the odds; are they reasonable, or almost impossible? What will happen if you guess wrong? A love affair gone awry, a lifelong relationship ruptured, a minor setback or a major tragedy?

You might keep in mind that people who specialize in working with the dying report that their patients almost never say, "I will always regret that I took that trip to Crete . . . changed jobs . . . married Emily . . ." What they do say is, "If I had it to do over again, I would have gone to Hawaii, given myself a year to see if I could make it as a sculptor, asked Maria for a date, tried that exciting job."

People who are dying, that is, are concerned far more with the things they were afraid to do than with those they did do, even though some of the things they did try didn't work out.

If you *really* want something, try for it. Just be sure that you have looked inside yourself with as much honesty and as much insight as you can master; do you really want to be rich? famous? married? Or do you just think you ought to want those things?

One of John's clients was in her early thirties; what she wanted was to be married and have several children. She had always worked at places where most of the other employees were women. She was active in church — but only in the women's group. She liked to sew, to knit, and to embroider. She spent her vacations with her aging parents.

John suggested that if she really were serious about wanting to get married, she would have to make some major changes in her life: take a job (even if the prestige and the pay were lower) in some industry where most of her co-workers would be male; work on mixed committees at her church; take some classes which had more men than women.

It turned out, in spite of her previous lifestyle, that she really was serious about wanting to get married. Within a year she had married a widower with two small children, and was pregnant herself. She had to take sizeable risks to achieve her goal, but she did it.

This client is very pleased with John, her husband, her new children, and her pregnancy; most important, she is very pleased with herself. She took a risk — several risks, for that matter — and the gamble paid off. This doesn't always happen, of course; a risk is a risk because you can't count on the outcome.

On the other hand, maybe you might as well take risks, because sometimes even a sure thing doesn't pay off. Jeanne and Harney are fiscal conservatives. Their assets are in mutual funds, in a credit union (guaranteed 9%), in money market certificates of deposit. Except for this $3,100 that they invested a few years back in a stock that had no way to go but up. That 100 shares is now palely loitering in the vicinity of $12.50 a share, and shows no indication of ever getting back to $31, much less rising above that.

No profit in money, no psychic satisfaction, not even the thrill of knowing that they were taking a risk!

John is a born risk-taker. He started his career working full time at a mental health center. Before very long, it became obvious that the director was competent, well-liked, and not all that old; and that John's chances of promotion were not only low, but nil, until the director died or retired; there just wasn't anyplace else to go. So John went into teaching. For the first full year, John's sense of self-worth was in constant jeopardy. He was supposed to be the authority; whenever a student challenged a theory or even acted bored, John's anxiety rose. That all turned out well; John has been teaching for a good many years now, and he knows he's good at it (that doesn't keep him from the occasional alarm when one of his students challenges him, but the pangs are pretty minor now, compared to what they used to be).

His more recent ventures include this book and a game called "Gone Bananas." The game evolved over several years and is presently in its third incarnation. It is based on modified Freudian psychology. He invested time, money, and effort in the game (and it takes more money than you might think to test-market a game — or anything else). It will, of course, make John happy if the game eventually makes some money, becomes to psychology what "Monopoly" was to economics, or even enthralls a fairly limited number of people. The important thing, to John, is that it is now a good game. Inventing a game and marketing it is a risky thing to do; financially, he could make a lot more money by spending his time doing aptitude and interest testing. But that isn't risky; it's a sure thing.

Working on the game involved risk — and John found that the money involved was minor compared to the psychic risk. As long as he was working on the game in the privacy of his home, things were simple. When he began handing out prototypes to friends to play and criticize, the risk was greater. And when he did the first test marketing, his ego was really on the line.

Whether or not his creation will repay its investment in terms of money, we don't yet know. But John knew he needed to take the risk as another form of self-expression.

It has already repaid its psychic investment; it is a good game, and that's what is most important for him. So the risk has already paid off in that way, no matter what may happen to the game in the future.

Risk-taking, sensible risk-taking, should be more like poker or bridge than rolling dice. That is, you should have a reasonable idea of what the odds are, what cards you hold, what cards other people may be holding — just how big, that is, your risk really is.

Take Las Vegas gamblers. There are the people who spend a week or two as a vacation, who set aside a certain amount of money for gambling, counting it as part of their recreation budget. When it's gone, it's gone, and that's that. They limit the risk they are willing to take.

Then there are the compulsive gamblers, who are a very different breed. Their compulsion happens to be gambling, but they are very similar to alcoholics or heroin addicts in many ways. Most of them will admit that they know the odds are against them (why else would Las Vegas exist?) but while they are gambling they manage to space this knowledge out. They get intermittent reinforcement — if you gamble long enough, even in Las Vegas, you are going to win occasionally — and so they keep on. If they are winning, they keep on to win more; if they are losing, they keep on to get even.

These people — like many people who are addicted to something other than gambling — tend to be self-centered, tense, nervous and anxious. Except when they are gambling when they tend to be overconfident, they are pessimistic and brooding. They are frustrated with their lack of achievement in real life. They like to think of themselves as taking well-calculated risks, but they know — really — and will even admit that they know the odds are heavily against them. That sort of gambling is not what we mean by ego-enhancing risk-taking; that sort of gambling is self-destruction.

With the economy in its present uncertain state,

millions of people who would never dream of turning up in Las Vegas or Atlantic City are gambling — putting their money in diamonds, platinum, Florida swamps, Colorado deserts, or krugerrands — without enough information to qualify their investments as reasonable risk-taking; what they are really doing is gambling in the roll-of-the-dice rather than the bridge or poker sense.

Inflation is scary; of course it is. But try, when you are taking your risks in the economic area, to decide, first, what your goals are; and second, how much of a risk are you really taking?

Risk, in whatever arena — physical, economic, or psychic — is exciting; it gives you a feeling of being alive, of meeting challenges. If you succeed, it gives you a sense of power, control, even, sometimes, omnipotence. Just be sure how much you have riding on that roll of the dice, that turn of the cards, that acceptance or rejection or career change.

Clearly, there are some things that you will decide are not worth risking. A loving, long term relationship for a passing infatuation (but is it really infatuation, or is it love? how do you know it's passing?) A promising career for a moment's angry outburst (but was that anger really how you have felt all along about your employer? Would you be better off changing now while you're still reasonably young and flexible?)

What you have to do is develop a sense of perspective. Ask yourself, when you are considering any major change in your life, whether what you *may* get out of it is worth what you *are* giving up. But remember that your psyche is made up of both rational and emotional components. Get in touch — really in touch — with your own feelings. If your emotions persist over a long time, maybe you should move in the direction of change even though your choice is not a "logical" one. Draw up a mental balance sheet, but don't base it either entirely on emotions or entirely on rational thought. The important thing is the sense of perspective, the balance between feelings and thoughts.

Life, inevitably, is full of choices. Life, equally inevitably, is full of risks. The trick is to recognize the risks, evaluate them, and make what you hope are the right choices — most of the time. You won't, of course, make the right choices all of the time. Nobody ever has.

Certainly there will be times when a risk is too great for the possible payoff. But only you can tell how risky a given venture feels to you. (If you're married, the decision should ideally be a mutual one; or at least, the more conservative spouse should have some sort of security blanket in the form of a time limit, a money limit — something to fall back on in case things don't work out).

Jeanne and Harney had been married for about a year and a half, working in Chicago, when Harney suggested that they should move to Denver. They came out on vacation, Harney found a job, and they moved. Then they looked around for a house they could afford to buy, and that incorporated some energy-saving features such as double-glazed windows, radiant heating, and lots of south-facing glass. There weren't any. So they bought a piece of alfalfa field in a Denver suburb (it's built up now, but it was wide open space then.) No natural gas, no water line, no sewer line, not even a road. They spent some months reading architectural journals, books on design, and how-to-do-your-own-plumbing manuals. And then they built a house.

This whole thing, to Jeanne's Chicago relatives, looked like sheer insanity. They had to look at an atlas to find out where Denver was, to begin with, and the idea of building your own house out in what they firmly believed was cowboy, if not Indian, territory, struck them as, well, less than sensible. Harney, it is true, had built a bird house once when he was in sixth grade, but Jeanne had never encountered a more primitive situation than the time the storm sewer got overloaded and backed up into the basement. All the streets in Chicago were paved (they had potholes, perhaps, but they were paved). Water is what you got by turning on a faucet. You heated your house with oil or gas, and if you didn't have a pipeline or a delivery truck, where were you?

Jeanne and Harney still live in the house and still like it. They are currently adding a solar greenhouse. The whole thing — which seemed so risky to Jeanne's relatives — never did feel risky to them, even when Harney's company went through a cost-cutting spasm and fired all the research people, including him. They lived on savings and Jeanne's job (until she had the baby) and kept on building the house. Everything worked out pretty well; they have city services now (not great, but more or less adequate), the kids enjoyed growing up in Colorado, and Harney and Jeanne are certainly glad they did it.

Risk, as we said earlier, is quite idiosyncratic.
The one really wrong choice is to choose to cut your risks to a minimum — to decide, on all occasions, not to take a risk.

Just keep in mind all those people on their deathbeds. Now that their freedom of choice is cut off, now that they are no longer in a position to decide whether to take a risk or to opt for safety, security and immobility — most of them wish that they had taken more, rather than fewer, risks when the option was there.

For it is only by taking risks that you have a chance of feeling like a winner, of feeling that instead of merely existing, you are growing, changing, improving — really *living*.

And even when the risk doesn't pay off — and sometimes it won't — you are likely to have gained more in both self-knowledge and a sense of adventure than you have lost.

To be . . . or not to be . . .

Why Don't You Listen to
What I'm Trying to Say?

Why Don't You Listen to What I'm Trying to Say?

(Communication)

Everybody knows how important it is to communicate with others, especially with our nearest and dearest. The trouble is that when you get much above the level of, "I just bit down on an olive pit and part of my tooth broke off. Do you think Dr. Carlson could squeeze me in soon?", communication is fraught with overtones and usually with difficulties.

Even a five year old who says, "Mama, could I have a glass of milk now?" may, depending on the circumstances, be saying: (1) I'm thirsty and milk sounds good; (2) you are paying too much attention to the baby and I want you to be paying attention to me; (3) I know lunch is going to be ready in ten minutes, but I don't think I'm going to like what you're fixing; (4) have you got over being mad at me because I drew pictures on my bedroom wall with your best nail polish? (5) — well, you can fill in the rest yourself.

Communication, whether it be verbal or non-verbal, is a two-way street: you have to try to send out clear signals, and you also have to be sensitive to the reactions of the person with whom you are trying to communicate. To illustrate one of the reasons that communication may be less than perfect, we are going to give you a little scenario: we're going to follow four people as they go on a picnic.

Theodore and Sandra Ferguson and Felix and Ingrid Sanford all work for the same large paint company. Theodore is a research chemist; Sandra is in charge of the billing department; Felix is a salesman (although his real love, which he pursues three evenings a week, is heading encounter groups); and Ingrid is an artist in the advertising department.

Theodore and Sandra are in their kitchen. Sandra says, "Theo, dear, would you mind moving a little to your left? I want to get the mustard out."

"Are you sure you don't think it would be better to have a steak fry? Sandwiches aren't nearly as interesting, although, of course, if it rains, it would be easier to eat them in the car. What if it does rain? Should we take the tarp along? I think maybe I'll go and get it."

"A steak fry would be fun, but the Forest Service still has a ban on open fires, so I don't think it would be very practical, Theo. I have all the sandwiches made, and I think they'll be just fine. After all, the food is only part of a picnic; it's the getting up into the mountains and away from the apartment. Anything tastes better in the open air."

"Well, all right, if you say so, but I do think I should go and look for the tarp, don't you?"

"It's in the trunk of the Datsun. I put it there last night."

"The Datsun? That's not going to be big enough, is it? Don't we want to take the folding chairs? And the table? If we go up to Summit Lake there won't be any picnic tables. And what if it really rains hard, Sandra? Maybe we should take the big tent and the Coleman lantern."

"If the Sanfords don't get here pretty soon, it's going to be too late for lunch; we'll have to make it a picnic supper. But we're not going up as far as Summit Lake, Theo; that's just not practical. We'll go to Echo Lake, and this early in the year, there are sure to be plenty of picnic tables. If it rains hard, we'll eat in the car, and hope we have better luck next time. Why do you have to make such a big deal out of everything?"

"Well, I just want to think of all the contingencies. It would be a shame to spoil a nice get-together by not having some little thing along."

"Little thing! Theo, if we took everything you've thought of this morning, we'd have to hire a U-Haul trailer. Let's just keep everything simple. Come and have another cup of coffee while we wait for Felix and Ingrid. I've got everything under control now."

"Sandra, do you realize that you have used the word 'everything' three times in the past fifteen seconds? Why do you have to be so — so enveloping always?"

Sandra giggles a little defensively. "I guess I should improve my vocabulary. It's just that I like to look at the whole package — to feel that everything (there's that word again, isn't it?) is going the way it should be. You know yourself that I'm the best billing manager they've ever had, and I think that's why. I keep track of the whole picture, the over-all operation, and let other people worry about the details."

Theo senses a criticism here. "That may be all right for something cut and dried, like billing, but I can't do my job that way. I have to pay attention to details, be alert to little things. Did I tell you I don't think that new acrylic resin is going to work out? It darkens the chrome yellow. I wish they weren't so infernally impatient to get new paints on the line; I need at least another month to check out some possible side reactions. I think that X7C50 formulation is going to be better than the last one, but I'd like to try—"

"Excuse me, dear; there's somebody at the door. Let's hope it's Felix and Ingrid."

It is Felix and Ingrid. Ingrid says blithely, "I'm so

199

sorry we're late, dear, of course it's my fault. I looked at the light coming through the Russian olive onto the patio this morning, and I thought, you know, that is really making a *statement* — a relevant statement, you know, and I just couldn't tear myself away until I got it down. Or partly down, anyway. Felix simply dragged me away. I hope I can recapture my feeling tomorrow. I have to wait until the light is right again."

Felix says, "Sandra, Theo, I'm sorry we're late. But you know how it is with creative people. I do apologize for keeping you waiting — Sandra, you're looking particularly lovely today, is that a new blouse? — but I didn't want Ingrid to lose her moment of inspiration."

"Well, you're here now," says Sandra. "Put the lemonade in the Datsun and let's get going."

"Lemonade?" says Felix blankly.

"Lemonade?" says Ingrid. "Oh, dear, I did promise to bring lemonade, didn't I?

"*I,*" Sandra says icily, "did not buy any lemons, because I expected you to bring the lemonade. I will make some instant tea, which is not as good as brewed iced tea, because we do not have time to wait for it to cool. Meanwhile, why don't you carry out the picnic basket and climb into the Datsun?"

There is a brief, embarrassed silence. Felix says, "Um, I don't think we'll fit in the Datsun. Ingrid has her painting things, you see. I'm afraid we'll have to use your station wagon. I'm terribly sorry, but these things happen, don't they? Why don't we just all relax and go with the flow?"

Theo has vanished and can be heard taking things from the Datsun and putting them into the station wagon. After considerable clanking and jingling noise, he reappears and remarks sheepishly, "As long as we're taking the big car anyway, I stuck in the lawn chairs and the folding table and the Coleman lantern. I do like to be prepared for whatever might happen."

Everyone is finally stuffed into the station wagon. Sandra fastens her seat belt, checks the rear view mirror, and remarks, "Ingrid, you're going to have to do something about that canvas. I can't see past it." Felix holds the canvas.

The trip to Echo Lake is not a chatty one. Sandra concentrates on driving. Ingrid looks dreamily out the window. Theo is brooding about Sandra's uncharitable attitude toward his paraphernalia. After all, one ought to be prepared. The chairs and table will be needed if all the picnic tables are already taken; the tarpaulin will be needed if there is a sudden rainstorm (true, the sky seen through the windshield is absolutely cloudless, but one never knows about weather in the mountains); the Coleman lantern will be needed if there is a sudden eclipse. Theo pulls himself together; even in a fantasy, he realizes that there is no such thing as an unexpected eclipse. Felix is well aware of the strained atmosphere; he tries a few remarks which fall flat, and relapses into silence, thinking that Sandra would benefit from an encounter group and that he must make an occasion to talk privately to Theo; poor Theo is always quiet, but today he is more subdued than ever.

Sandra pulls into a parking space. "There's a nice picnic table right there. Let's take it, shall we?"

Ingrid says brightly, "Sandra, dear, I know we can't all have the true artist's eye, but do you really want to be quite so close to the road? I'm sure we can find a place that's more aesthetically pleasing if we go on just a little."

Sandra grits her teeth and pulls out of the parking space. "All right, Ingrid, tell me when to stop."

Seven miles later, Ingrid says, "Oh, isn't this lovely! Stop, Sandra."

"No place to pull off. I'll have to go on."

Half a mile downhill, Sandra finds a shoulder wide enough to park on. Ingrid takes off briskly back toward the spot she has chosen. Felix carries her painting gear, saying apologetically, "Sorry I can't help with the other stuff. Just take what you can, and I'll come back for the rest." Sandra says, "Let's leave the chairs and table, and just take the food."

Felix brightens. "Good idea, Sandra. Get in touch with Mother Nature. We'll sit on the ground." He pauses thoughtfully. "No, Ingrid doesn't like sitting on the ground."

"Neither do I," says Theo. "Sandra, can you take one end of this table?"

The little procession makes its way up the hill to Ingrid, who says, "Whatever took you so long? This is a superb view, isn't it? But somehow I don't feel inspired to do a landscape. I'll do a still life instead. Sandra, if you'll put the iced tea jug just *there,* and the fruit in front of it, and if we unwrap the sandwiches — look at the lovely angle the bread makes with the apricots."

"You can have ten minutes, Ingrid," says Sandra. "Any more than that, and the sandwiches are going to curl up and be too dry to eat. I spent an hour this morning making them, and I don't intend to let them go to waste."

"Um," says Ingrid. "Just let me block in these forms."

Felix and Theodore go for a walk. Felix is concerned about his friend, and Theo finally says, "I don't know, Felix, Sandra's been putting me down all day. She does it more and more. Before we got married, I admired her because she was so efficient, so decisive. And she seemed to admire me because I'm so careful about details; said she'd never dated anybody before who was sure to be prepared for anything that came up. But lately, I don't know — we're beginning to drive each other up the wall."

"You've got to get in touch with your feelings, Theo," Felix says earnestly. "Try to communicate with Sandra. If you can't do it on your own, why don't you come to one of my encounter groups? You'd be amazed at some of the changes I see in people after just two or three sessions."

"I don't know, Felix. I never have liked the idea of sitting around and spilling my guts to a bunch of strangers. I even have trouble talking to one person at a time — about things that I feel, I mean; I don't mind talking about *ideas*."

Twenty minutes pass. The two men stroll back to the picnic area. Ingrid is saying, "Just another couple of minutes and I'll have enough down to remember it. I do want to catch the contrast of those purple grapes with the bread — you see how the bread looks almost gray in this light?"

"It isn't the light," says Sandra in a carefully even voice, "it's rye bread, and it's turning gray because it's drying out. In fact, it has finished drying out."

Felix says anxiously, "Now. Sandra, dear, don't get so upset. If you would just go with the flow — get in touch — really in touch — with your feelings—"

Sandra's voice is not quite so carefully controlled. "I believe I am already in touch with my feelings, Felix. The primary feeling I have at the moment is sheer, primitive fury. I am now going to walk down to the car, and when I get there I am going to open the flask of brandy that we keep in the first aid kit, and I am going to drink the whole thing. And somebody else can pack up the stuff and carry it back and drive the damn car down the damn mountain."

Now, what in the world is the matter with these people?

The late great psychoanalyst Carl G. Jung would have had the answer: the four people on the picnic are operating according to four separate aspects of psychological orientation. To put it in a more contemporary American idiom, they're all coming from different places; and they don't appreciate — in fact, they dislike — each others' world views.

Jungian Functions

Jung theorized that the human mind has four functions: sensation; thinking; feeling; and intuition. (This may sound tidier in German, the language in which Jung wrote; we don't know.) Anyway, Jung believed that, at birth, all four functions are equally present, but that soon afterwards, everybody chooses one to be the major way of relating to the world, suppresses the opposite function, and uses the other two as ancillary (helping) ways of understanding the world. Thinking, in the Jungian view, is the opposite of feeling, and sensation is the opposite of intuition.

In terms of internal psychological dynamics, this would mean that if you consciously view the world from a thinking point of view, your unconscious mind is simply seething with feelings.

In terms of relating to other people, it would mean that you not only do not understand people whose world view, or way of functioning, is the opposite of yours; you tend to dislike them, or to have a feeling that their mode of operating is flaky, perverse, or downright wrongheaded.

Thinking Theodore

The thinking person, as Jung used the term, relates to the world analytically. This seems rather sensible at first glance, but it (like all the other types) has its drawbacks. The closer you are to a pure thinking type, the harder it is for you to make a decision: you tend to get hung up on details, and to want to have *all* the facts before you decide anything. Like Theo, you want to be prepared for all possible contingencies. Since the world is not set up to provide *all* the facts in any given situation, people simply must make decisions on a selection of facts; for some people this is easy, but for Jungian thinking types it is very difficult indeed.

Thinking people are good at research. They do not make good politicians. They make terrible presidents. Somebody in a position of power, whether it be political, or corporate, or some other kind of power, *has* to make decisions. The sort of person who has a longing for all the facts is in effect paralyzed when it comes to decisions; and even wrong decisions (everybody makes some wrong decisions) are better than no decision at all.

Sensate Sandra

Sensate people are practical, efficient, and great at organization. If they head a committee, a department, a company, they may not be universally loved — because they tend to get impatient with people who are less efficient than they are, and show it — but they are likely to be respected.

Sandra, if she is ambitious enough, is likely to wind up as head of the firm, or to found a company of her own. And she, unlike any of the other people on the picnic, will be great at it. Each of these people is good at his or her own job, but only the sensate person, who is quick at seeing the overall picture, does not hesitate to make changes if necessary, is not particularly concerned with sentiment or with being liked by one and all, is going to make a really good major executive.

This is not to say that executives have to be insensitive clods: it is to say that if you are in a position of considerable power you have to be clearsighted as to alternative choices, and you have to be able to make important decisions without dithering around.

Feeling Felix

Feeling people are very sensitive to other people. They spend their lives being more aware of interpersonal relationships, both more troubled and more satisfied by them, than most people do. A feeling person could be described, perhaps, as Freud's ideal woman: self-sacrificing, subservient, intensely aware of other people's needs, and willing to go to great lengths to make other people happy.

Felix is a good salesman because he really pays attention to his customers' needs, and they sense his interest and concern for their well-being, and respond by giving him their business. He is good at running encounter groups for the same reason; everybody comes away feeling better after a meeting with Felix.

Felix gets something out of all this effort on other people's behalf; he enjoys helping people, and he basks in their response to him. The danger with feeling people is that they may never really know who they themselves are: that is, they spend so much psychic effort on pleasing other people that they don't stop to consider what they, themselves, want.

Intuitive Ingrid

Intuitive people have given the world some of its lasting works of art. And they have given their families some of their major headaches. Intuitive people tend to be creative, sometimes to the point of obsession, and they have a blithe faith that the whole world ought to see that their creations are as important as they themselves know they are. If the world doesn't appreciate them, that's the world's loss; and if their families are not eager to sacrifice themselves for the sake of the artist — or to be more precise, for the sake of the artist's art — well, there must be something wrong with the other people.

Ingrid is lucky to be married to Felix, who wants to please her (as well as everybody else) and who genuinely admires her talent. But she is going to have to modify her singlemindedness a bit if she wants to keep any friends. Perhaps, being Ingrid, she won't mind if she loses them all; her art, to Ingrid, really is of consuming importance.

Functioning with Jung's Functions

Nobody, of course, is a really pure Jungian type; people are mixtures. But if you find yourself taking an instant dislike to a new acquaintance, you might consider whether he or she is operating largely from a function opposite to yours. If so, keep in mind that neither you nor the other person can help it: mind-sets of this sort begin so early in life that they are not a matter of choice once you get older. If you can't *like* another person's way of functioning, perhaps you can at least understand it, and if at all possible, respect it.

This is particularly important if the other person concerned is your spouse. During courtship, opposites often are attracted to each other (like Theo and Sandra). However, when the honeymoon is over, the very traits which seemed so charming in a lover may be the ones which are so maddening in a husband or wife.

If the two of you think alike, your marriage may be smoother — but there is much more potential for growth if you have different ways of functioning. The vital thing is to respect your spouse's way of relating to the world, even if you don't really understand it. (This does not apply to value judgments; if you discover that your spouse is cheating in ways that are important to you — whether it be income tax or sexual fidelity or anything else you care about — get things straightened out).

But if you are, for instance, a sensate man (well organized, decisive, wanting to be in charge of things) married to an intuitive woman (creative, obsessed with her work, and indifferent to such mundane affairs as dinner on the table and buttons on shirts) you are both going to have to work hard to keep a good marriage, but you can each learn from the other, and your marriage can be far more interesting than most people's.

Non-Verbal Communication

Probably more than half of all the communication that takes place between people is non-verbal. The student who leans back in her seat, folds her arms across her chest, and gazes sullenly out the window, yawning from time to time, is telling the lecturer something which he or she would rather not know. The man who fumbles for his wallet just long enough to let his dinner partner say, "Oh, that's all right; I'll get it this time," may be expressing his resentment at having paid for dinner the last six times he and his acquaintance got together, or he may feel that these business dinners work out more to his partner's advantage than to his. In any case, he is expressing his feelings rather eloquently without saying a word. The elderly couple who walk down the street holding hands, the friends whose eyes meet in amusement during a lecture, the mother who slams her toddler into a grocery cart — all are using non-verbal communication.

The Double Bind

Double bind communication can be verbal, non-verbal or a combination. The essence of double bind messages is that the recipient is always in a no-win situation. There is the kindergarten art teacher who tells the class that they should draw whatever they feel like, and then says, "Sarah, that's not a very happy picture, is it? Take another piece of paper and try again." There is the parent who indicates that a child's allowance is his to spend just as he likes, and then explodes when he buys a punk rock record with it. There is the mother who gives her son two sweaters for his birthday, and when he wears the red one the next morning, says, "What's the matter? You didn't like the blue one?"

Double bind messages spring from ambivalence on the part of the sender. (Do you know Bennet Cerf's definition of ambivalence? The feeling you have when you see your mother-in-law driving your brand new sports car off the cliff.) If you want to come across to your neighbors as the always-loving, tenderly nurturing parent, and you have just changed into your best dry-clean-only dress, and your four year old daughter comes charging across the yard covered with mud and clearly bent on a loving embrace — that's ambivalence.

In order to refrain from sending double bind messages, you must first clarify your own thinking. Do you really want your kindergarten class to express their own feelings, or do you want them to produce only happy pictures, thus indicating to their parents that you are one of the world's outstanding educators of the very young? Do you really believe that allowances belong to the recipient, or do you believe that the young should defer to your superior judgment when it comes to turning money into goods? Examine your own motives: what do you *really* want to communicate? If you keep sending double bind messages to your children, if you keep telling them to be independent but actually exercise too much control over their lives, they are going to feel untrustworthy or incompetent, and given the wrong heredity and a precipitating factor or two, they may even turn schizophrenic. And you surely don't want that if you can help it.

Good communication implies clarity. And to send a clear message, you must first look inside your own head and decide what message you truly want to send. And then you hope that the person with whom you are trying to communicate will listen to what you are trying to say.

To paraphrase a well known saying: "I know you think you think you heard what I said. But what I think you think I said is not what I meant." In other words, sending out clear messages can indeed be troublesome at times. But keep on trying; it really is worth the effort.

Cuddle Up a Little Closer

Cuddle Up a Little Closer
(Intimacy)

Pam and Jerry haven't seen each other for a week; Pam, who is co-owner of a small bookstore in Denver, has been on a buying trip to San Francisco. Pam lets herself in to the apartment and makes her way to the den, guided by the sound of a television commercial.

"Hello, dear," she says. "I did think perhaps you would meet me at the airport."

"Pam," says her husband, "the *series* is on! How would it look to the customers tomorrow if the manager of the Winken Sporting Goods couldn't talk about what happened to the Phillies in the seventh? Listen, there's just a few more minutes left of this inning; why don't you go unpack or something?"

"During the next commercial, you might do something about those empty beer cans," Pam says acidly. "I can hardly see the surface of the coffee table."

When the game, the instant replays of highlights, and the locker room interviews are finally over, Pam and Jerry rendezvous in the kitchen for a cheese sandwich and a glass of milk.

"Did you get hold of the man about the kitchen counters?" Pam asks. "I'm pretty tired of this mess."

"He's coming at ten Wednesday morning."

"Wednesday! But that's Carla's day off! I can't stay home on a Wednesday."

"Why don't you just close the store? I haven't noticed

you raking in enough profit to make much of a difference, anyway."

"Never mind, I'll call and see if I can get him to make it Thursday instead. I think I'm catching a cold; it was really chilly on the coast."

"I've been limping for the last three days. Some idiot dropped a bowling ball on my foot. I'm afraid I'm going to lose the nail on my big toe."

Pam rinses the glasses and puts the rest of the cheese away. "Would you like me to sleep in the guest room until your foot is better?"

"No way! I got hit with a bowling ball, not a bomb!"

Vera and Tom haven't seen each other for a week, either. Vera is co-owner of another small bookstore in Denver, and she, too, has been on a buying trip to San Francisco. Vera lets herself in, and makes her way to the kitchen, guided by the sound of a power drill.

"Vera, honey!" says Tom. Your plane isn't due for three hours and forty minutes yet. What are you doing home so early? Not that I'm not glad to see you."

"I knew you'd want to watch the game tonight, so I traded tickets with Nancy. She said she'd just as soon have one more meal in San Francisco anyway. Oh — you're redoing the counters. You must have spent every spare minute I've been gone working on them. They look absolutely gorgeous."

"Well, they took longer than I thought they would, but I'm almost finished. This corner is the trickiest bit, see?"

"I'm really impressed. I thought you were going to have the store install them."

"I was, but they couldn't get here for a couple of weeks, and I wanted to surprise you. Well, tell me all about your trip. Was the coat warm enough? I've looked at the San Francisco weather reports every evening, and I worried about you."

"It was a little chilly, but I was inside a lot of the time, of course. Oh, darling, I heard Isaac Asimov speak; I do wish you could have heard him too. And you remember that little Lebanese restaurant by Golden Gate Park? I had lunch there today, and I got to thinking how much fun we had there the last time we went, and so I brought some of their special eggplant appetizer home with me, and some real sourdough bread. Let me get it out of my bag, and we'll eat it while we watch the game."

"That sounds great, but do you know what sounds even better? Why don't we just take it up to bed? We can always find out how the Phillies did tonight on the news tomorrow morning."

"Oh, come on — you know perfectly well that one of the reasons Blinken Sporting Goods thinks so much of you is that you can talk sports with the customers; watching the game tonight is really part of your job. It's just lucky that you like it so much."

"Maybe you're right. You're sure you're not too tired?"

"Don't be silly; I spent my afternoon sitting on a plane, not working on the kitchen counters. That is such a beautiful job you did — I can't get over how professional it looks. It was so sweet of you to want to surprise me with it."

"All the while I was working on it I was thinking of how you would look when you saw it. Do you know that for me half the fun of doing anything is thinking about your reaction to it?"

"You really are a darling. I missed you — even in San Francisco."

"Let's go turn on the TV, and every time the game gets dull, you can tell me about your trip."

Both these couples enjoy *physical* intimacy; only Vera and Tom have *emotional* intimacy as well. Pam and Jerry may never have had it, or they may be going through a stage in their relationship where they simply are not in close rapport with each other. Each of them is almost completely concerned with his or her own needs, and indifferent to the needs of the other. Vera and Tom, on the other hand, are deeply aware of each other's interests, concerns, feelings, and sensitive to them.

Everybody needs both physical and emotional intimacy, but the need for each varies among individuals and, for each person, may vary from time to time. Although this chapter is concerned mainly with intimacy among adults, we would like to point out that emotional intimacy is a need of children, too. The physical intimacy which is, perhaps, the only kind an infant is aware of, grows into an emotional bond. As children grow older, they need emotional intimacy, first with their parents, then with other children.

This is an essay which John's daughter, Jenny, wrote when she was in seventh grade: "Being a desk is not my idea of fun, actually. It's not so bad when a small seventh grader sits in you but when a ninth grade football player is sitting in you it can get tiring. Especially after forty-five minutes. It can also get boring at night or summer. Thank goodness there are other desks to talk to. But their old stories do get tiresome about the good old days when they were new. And when some joker comes in and moves you around! Now that makes me mad. You spend all night moving around to get next to your friends."

People of Jenny's age need friends; more especially, they need at least one friend in whom they can confide absolutely anything, whom they can trust with any secret, whose love they can count on unconditionally. That is not a need which goes away as one gets older: you may be able to do without physical intimacy for long periods of time, but if you aren't emotionally intimate with at least one person — relative, friend, lover, spouse — many of your needs will go unmet.

Physical intimacy

According to a recent survey, most *men* equate physical intimacy with having intercourse. Most *women* feel that, while intercourse may be the culminating act, kissing, cuddling, hugging, even holding hands are an important part of physical intimacy. As a group, women are more inclined than men to want emotional intimacy intertwined with physical intimacy — or at least they are more capable of expressing these feelings than are most men. It is our belief that whether you are male or female, you can have the greatest sex life in the world, and if you don't have emotional intimacy, you will feel empty and unsatisfied.

Physical intimacy can sometimes lead to emotional intimacy, but it won't necessarily do so. Emotional intimacy is more likely to lead to physical intimacy; in this case, the physical intimacy is more an expression of the emotional rapport than a thing apart.

Emotional intimacy

There are, of course, degrees of emotional intimacy. With few exceptions, or perhaps no exceptions, long-term relationships have their ups and downs. There are times when partners can read each other's minds, and there are times when the same partners will feel they must have been absolutely deranged to have believed they had anything at all in common with the other person.

Most women have a friend, or a handful of friends, with whom they are on confidential terms. It is highly satisfying to have a cup of tea and a bitter conversation about what is wrong with one's husband — but you'd better be sure about just how emotionally intimate you and your friend are. Can you count on her to understand that this is a temporary aberration on your part? That you still love your husband, maddening though he is at the moment? That what you are telling her about his inconsiderateness not only should go no further, but should be tactfully forgotten in the near future?

And can she count on you in the same way?

Most women do have someone to whom they can confide almost anything. Most men, unfortunately, do not. Men in our society (although this is changing) form friendships on the basis of common professional or recreational interests rather than on mutual emotional support. Emotional intimacy, for men, may come only through marriage, or it may not come at all.

Loneliness

Loneliness is not to be confused with solitude. Everybody (this, like everything, varies from person to person) needs some time to be alone; emotional intimacy has nothing to do with "togetherness" in the sense of spending every possible moment together. Emotional intimacy implies that you do enjoy each other's company — but nobody can enjoy somebody else's company every waking moment.

It's all right for each of you to enjoy doing things apart from each other. He jogs, you play bridge; she climbs mountains, you collect stamps. Neither of you is lonely when you are doing separate things.

Loneliness is something else. If you feel a lack of emotional intimacy, you can be lonely although your partner is sitting across the dinner table from you, talking to you, or even making love to you.

Loneliness leads to estrangement, and that in turn can lead to depression.

Avoiding intimacy

Intimacy is one of the great joys, the great necessities, of the human condition. Why, then, do some people avoid it?

Fear is the most common reason. Not exactly fear of rejection, though that may enter into it, so much as fear of being misunderstood, or of losing the respect of your partner. If you have fantasies which you have never expressed to your partner or anybody else, you may well feel it is the better part of valor to shut up about them, even though disclosing your private fears and visions is the road to increased intimacy. If your own self-image is a little shaky, you may fear that your partner, once you have revealed your innermost thoughts and feelings, will know you all too well — and who could continue to love anybody like the real, private you?

If you have been involved in an intimate relationship which ended in a bitter break-up, you may be feeling like a once-burned child: twice shy. People recovering from a divorce may feel very ambivalent about becoming intimate with somebody new. On the one hand, they desperately need to feel loved and understood; on the other hand, they are terribly vulnerable and reluctant to leave themselves open to rejection or even mere indifference.

Our advice is to take it easy, but don't give up. If you have just emerged from a disastrous break-up — even if you were the one who initiated it — you are, for the time being, not a good judge of people. If you are a woman, you may oscillate between being convinced that all men are as despicable as the one from whom you have just parted, and believing that since nobody else could possibly be that bad, you have nowhere to go but up. You may be so starved for affection, or for reassurance as to your own attractiveness, that you will settle for someone — anyone — who even hints at a desire for emotional intimacy.

Not only are you a poor judge of other people at a time like this, but you yourself are neither the person you were nor the person you will become once you have had a chance to catch your breath and regain your perspective. Any conversation between two victims of recently ended love affairs is likely to be a set of separate monologues rather than a real exchange of thoughts and feelings. Both of you want sympathy, and neither of you, for the time being, is capable of giving it.

Go ahead and socialize, but try not to make any long-term commitments until you have got your balance again.

Fostering intimacy

What if you haven't been through a traumatic break-up? What if you have a pleasant, comfortable relationship already, but feel you could use a bit more in the way of emotional intimacy? How do you foster intimacy?

Before you do anything at all, give some thought to the quality of the relationship as it is now. We all fantasize about a partner who says, "I love you," on all possible occasions, who calls twice a day from the office and three times a day if out of town, who never forgets an anniversary, and who turns up with charming little no-occasion gifts about once a week.

Hardly anybody, let us admit, has a partner like this — and if they did, they might find it emotionally wearing; nobody outside of a Gothic novel can sustain this level of attention for very long.

People's ability to express their feelings verbally varies widely. If your partner never, or hardly ever, *says* "I love you," you may indeed be lacking emotional intimacy. On the other hand, if that partner remembers your taste in food, colors, recreation, interests of any kind, and takes those tastes into consideration in spending time with you — just keep firmly in mind that strong, silent types have been much admired in American culture for several generations now. Don't nag.

If, however, your situation is more like that of Pam and Jerry at the beginning of this chapter, if you realize that you are leading parallel lives with very little interest in each other's concerns, what can you do? Well, you can decide to split and hope for better luck next time, or you can try to improve the situation — change your attitudes rather than your partner.

Remember that any long-term relationship is going to go through fallow periods, so to speak, and that it may get better again merely because of the passage of time. However, if you would like to hurry the process along a bit, you can probably do it. Any change that you make in your own way of life is going to produce a change of some sort in your partner's attitude toward you. It may not necessarily be the sort of change you were hoping for, since all change involves some risk. However, if you play your cards right, you are very likely to produce some improvement in intimacy.

Begin by listening. If there's nothing but silence to listen to, ask questions. Not "Why don't you ever talk to me any more?" but something on the order of, "Is Mr. Simmons any easier to get along with since he got back from his vacation?" If you have to start with, "How was your day?" so be it, but you might ask yourself if you've been paying as much attention to your partner's concerns as you wish your partner would pay to yours. You might do better with, "Tell me about your day, dear. We've been so busy with other things lately I feel we've lost touch a little with each other."

Emotional intimacy grows out of a continued exchange of *feelings*. If you are both very busy people, you may feel you're doing well if you can find time to arrive at a mutual decision on what color to paint the guest room or whether to have the avocado in salad tonight or let it ripen one more day and turn it into guacamole tomorrow or if Johnny should be tutored in math. How can you possibly find time for mutual soul-searching?

Actually, almost any subject, no matter how mundane, can serve as a springboard for increased emotional intimacy. Take the three examples above:

"I've always wanted to have a room with red walls and white carpeting, but I've never felt it would be practical. But the guest room wouldn't get much traffic; do you suppose it would be too silly—"

"I don't think so. That room needs a new carpet anyway, and we can tell the kids they have to take their shoes off if they want to go into it. Why do you think you feel so strongly about that color combination?"

"Oh, I know why I do. It was in a scene in a movie I saw when I was nine or ten. I can't remember anything about the plot or the characters, but I do remember thinking it was the most elegant room I'd ever seen in my life."

"Hey, if we turned the bed in the other direction, do you suppose we could fit your desk in there? Think how much more exciting it would be to figure the taxes in the most elegant room you've ever seen."

"This avocado feels all right for slicing, but it isn't soft enough for guacamole. What do you think?"

"Let's save it another day and make guacamole. We can pretend we're back in Santa Fe having dinner before the opera. Remember how it rained all afternoon, and then cleared in the evening?"

"I'll never forget that night. Such incredible music, and then such an incredible display of stars in the sky. We really ought to spend another weekend down there before too long."

"Johnny just doesn't seem to be getting the hang of algebra; he brought his report card home today and he has a C minus again. I've tried helping him but he hates the stuff so much he's beginning to hate me for making him think about it. Do you want to give it a try?"

"I wonder if we couldn't find somebody who's good in math and a year ahead of him, and have him tutored. I seem to remember when I was that age I learned things much faster from kids just a little older than I did from my parents."

"Me too. Why do you suppose that is?"

"Maybe because you want to feel independent of your parents, so you're annoyed when you have to accept their help."

"I suppose so. What do you think? Should we ask the school who might be willing to tutor him?"

"Or we could ask Johnny to find somebody."

"Good thought. I think he really knows he needs help, and if he got to pick the helper it might inspire him to buckle down and get the thing done. Oh, I'm so glad you thought of that. I've really been feeling — well, I guess you'd say inadequate — dealing with Johnny lately. He isn't the sweet little boy he used to be, and I don't think I'm very good at dealing with

223

adolescents."

"Nobody is very good at dealing with adolescents. You just have to hang in there and let all those emotional storms wear themselves out. You're doing fine, honey; some day Johnny will appreciate what a great parent you are, and I appreciate you right now."

The same three topics might, given another couple, lead to this conversation:

"Are you ever going to get around to painting the guest room?"

"I'll try to do it next weekend if you get the paint and the brushes."

"Why should I get the paint and the brushes? Every time I do you say there's something wrong with what I got. You do it yourself this time, and then you won't have anybody to blame but yourself."

"No, but you will. I did choose the color for Nancy's room, you remember, and you didn't speak to me for a week."

"Well, anybody who would paint the walls lavender when you knew perfectly well I had made a bedspread and curtains and cushions with red and orange flowers—"

"How was I supposed to know that?"

"Because I not only told you, but the material was lying around for days while I was working on it."

"I've gotten so used to things lying around for days that I try not to pay any attention to them."

"Oh, just do whatever you want to with the guest room, just as long as you get it done. Do you want me to put the avocado in the salad tonight, or save it for guacamole tomorrow?"

"Guacamole. It covers up the avocado taste. Why you insist on buying avocados when you know I don't like them—"

"When did you ever tell me you didn't like avocados?"

"I do it about once a month. You just don't listen very carefully."

"I do too. You just don't say things very clearly sometimes. I'll eat the avocado myself, then; I only bought it because it was on special sale, and you're always going on about the grocery bills."

"I see Johnny got another C minus in algebra. That kid never has learned how to study."

"He doesn't have much of an example, does he? When is the last time you read a book? Or anything but the sports page? If you're so concerned about his getting a better grade, why don't you help him with his homework for a change? I've about had it!"

"Well, if you've been helping him, maybe that explains his grade. Women never are any good at math."

"Hey, who's been doing the taxes around here for fifteen years? You can try doing them yourself next spring. And balancing the checkbook. And—"

Now, there is a lot of emotional content in this conversation; it's just not the right kind to promote emotional intimacy. Each partner is hostile to the other, and the hostility springs directly from the basic indifference which each feels for the concerns of the other. Each is feeling emotionally deprived, and instead of trying to improve the situation, to provide mutual support, each is lashing wildly out at the other, trying to prove that he or she is the martyr in the case.

That second conversation took at least as much time as the first one — and it isn't over yet. It could end tonight with one of them sleeping in the bedroom and the other in the still unpainted guest room, without having had the avocado or anything else for dinner.

The amount of time you spend on communicating with each other is not nearly as important as the quality: that is, are you demonstrating indifference, or are you affirming love, appreciation, concern, respect for each other?

Are we saying that if you want to have emotional intimacy, you should never criticize your partner?

No, indeed; emotional intimacy implies an open exchange of feelings, whether positive or negative. Nobody is perfect, neither you nor your partner. Each of you has a thing or two in mind which would improve the other. You can get this across, but you don't have to do it in a hostile way. If the proposed change is important to you, go ahead and talk about it, but be sure the situation holds as little threat as possible for the other person.

Possible opening gambits are, "It's hard for me to say this . . ."; "I don't know quite how to put this . . ."; "I feel we both should make some changes . . ." The most endearing version we've ever heard was said by a young man to one of Jeanne's daughters: "You understand that I love absolutely everything about you; but I think the thing I love *least* about you is . . ."

Emotional intimacy and your children

There are two angles to this: how do you teach your children to express their feelings and appreciate those of other people? and how do you and your spouse manage to get enough time, privacy, and energy to enrich your relationship with each other while raising children?

As to the first question, children learn best by example. If you want your children to be honest, you don't boast in their hearing about the cash deal you just made which isn't going to turn up on your income tax report. If you truly feel that income taxes are so unfair that you are justified in dealing a few hands under the table, you can explain that to them; but the childish mind being what it is, you shouldn't be surprised to have Betsy explain to you at some later date, "I know the teacher doesn't like me as well as she likes Barbara, because Barbara always gets better marks, so I thought it was OK to cheat on the English test." If you want your children to be courageous, you don't hide in the closet during a thunderstorm. You can tell them (they will know anyway) that you are always a little scared during storms, but that you know it is silly, and you are trying to get over it.

Similarly, if you want your children to become loving, caring adults capable of sharing feelings (in both directions) with other people, then you simply must yourself become, if you are not already, that kind of person. If you and your spouse have a good, open, loving relationship with each other, your children are going to take that as the norm, and look for it in their own encounters. If one of you is exploiting the other, or if you don't very much care about each other's feelings, your children are going to take *that* as the norm, and act accordingly.

As for sharing your feelings directly with your children, you can't in good conscience tell a five year old that you're worried sick that your husband is about to lose his job and that you will all be cast penniless out into the snow (even though it is now June and all the peonies are blooming splendidly outside the front door just now). You can say something like "I'm feeling a little sad right now, but I'll feel better soon. Would you rather have cheese or peanut butter for lunch? After lunch you can tell me all about how things went at kindergarten today."

When it comes to the second question about

emotional intimacy in a household with children, a lock on the bedroom door and firm understanding about bedtimes for the younger generation help a good deal. Beyond that, you simply have to *make* some time to be alone together, to talk about things that may not be suitable for very young ears, to remember how it was when there were just the two of you, to cherish the enrichment which children can bring to your lives, but also to reassure each other that the commitment which brought you together in the first place will continue when the children are grown and gone.

Commitment

Many people in the current young adult generation are accustomed to instant gratification. Emotional intimacy is not an instant phenomenon. It takes years to grow. You can have an instant interest, an instant rapport, an instant mutual desire. But emotional intimacy is more like a mosaic than a poured concrete sidewalk; it is made up of innumerable tiny pieces of memory, shared experiences, slow growth in appreciating each other, a certain tolerant fondness for each other's foibles, a trust and respect for each other.

It takes a long time. But it is well worth it. Living together without emotional intimacy is like eating an egg without salt: bland, at best.

Yipes! What's Happening to Me?

Yipes! What's Happening to Me?

(Mid-Life Crisis)

Harry and Janet have been married for almost eighteen years. They have three teenage children who are as amiable and problem-free as adolescents can be.

Janet is thirty-eight, and she has been spending her spare time lately working toward a realtor's license. She has been enjoying studying again — she left college in her junior year to marry Harry, and while she has never exactly regretted that step, she finds it fun and challenging to have to pass tests again. She has done her share of volunteer work through the years, but she thinks that what she really wants to do right now is prepare herself to earn some money. After all, the kids are going to be ready for college before they know it, and although Harry's income is a good one, anything she can add to it will help. Harry has been getting somewhat moody lately, though; when they talked over her plans a few months ago, he seemed to be all in favor of them. Now he's gotten a lot more picky about what she serves for dinner and whether all his shirts have all their buttons and are starched exactly the way he wants them to be. He was happy enough with synthetics for years, but now he wants genuine get-your-wife-to-iron-it natural materials. He's also concerned about whether she spends enough time riding herd on the children. Surely, their children, at thirteen, sixteen, and seventeen, could be called young adults. They've always been responsible youngsters (well, two out of three isn't bad, and Jerry has been improving lately). Why does Harry seem so unduly concerned all of a sudden? He heartily approved when she spent all those hours as a volunteer at the hospital, when she ran the church bake sales with such success, and such expenditure of time and effort, when she buttonholed everybody in the neighborhood to get that recall petition passed. She's home now as much as she usually was during the years the children were in elementary school. What's wrong?

Harry is forty-two, and he has been steadily climbing the corporate ladder for seventeen years, ever since he got his master's degree in business administration. He is now a second vice president in charge of development. He likes his job. Or perhaps, he reflects, he *used* to like his job. Somehow, ever since he got that last promotion, even though it was what he had been aiming for for years, work hasn't been as enjoyable as it used to be. He finds himself looking at the younger men in the office, wondering which bright young man (like himself seventeen or eighteen years ago) is going to try an end run around him. Who was it who first used the term "the rat race"? Whoever it was certainly had something there. He is feeling more and more like a rat trapped in a maze, with the cheese and the electric shock getting harder and harder to tell apart. Janet ought to appreciate all he's done for her all these years, instead of suddenly trying to build a separate life for herself. The kids were just getting into the most difficult phase of their lives, and she should realize that her place was where it always has been: right here at home.

Harry, who has dressed conservatively for the past two decades, suddenly buys himself a bright red jacket. He tells the barber not to clip his sideburns so short. He would grow a beard if it weren't for the awkward transition stage. Maybe on his next vacation, he thinks, he will start a beard and see how he likes it. He begins to find excuses to chat with the twenty year old receptionist as his younger colleagues do, forgetting that six months ago his main emotion when he thought of her was exasperation: her I.Q. hasn't improved noticeably since then, but somehow that no longer seems so important.

And one day Harry comes home and announces to a startled Janet that he wants a divorce. He is tired of his job, his home, his children, and her. She can have the house and the money they have saved for the children's education; as for him, he is going to take his share of their assets and spend a year finding himself. When he was in high school, he always thought he might like to be a painter. Now he's finally going to get out of the boring rut he has been in all these years and actually see if he can paint.

Has Harry lost his marbles?

No, just his perspective. Both Harry and Janet, in their different ways, are going through a mid-life crises. Janet is experiencing a period of growth which she sees as positive and reasonable. Harry is going through a time of general dissatisfaction with all phases of his life, and wants to change everything about it in the hope that some aspect of the change will give him the satisfactions he is looking for.

Mid-Life Crisis in Men

Mid-life crisis, like adolescence, is probably a universal phenomenon, part of the human condition. Like adolescence, it can be a smooth transition from one phase of life to the next — or at least a relatively smooth transition. Or it can be a traumatic event both for the sufferer and his family.

It is, in a sense, a modern "luxury." Most of our ancestors were far too busy trying to keep those bison or eland steaks coming to stop and consider whether they really felt fulfilled, and far fewer of them even reached the ripe old age of forty or fifty.

Now, life is full of deadlines. If you don't begin studying ballet before you are in your middle teens, you may as well forget about ever being anything but a member of the chorus. If you learn to play tennis when you're thirty you are unlikely ever to be invited to Wimbledon except as a member of the audience. You can't become a concert violinist without years of early endeavor behind you.

Somehow, however, the deadlines which present themselves to men somewhere between their late thirties and early fifties seem particularly frightening. So many options seem about to be cut off. If you want to change your job, you'd better do it now — you've noticed that personnel managers seem to be getting younger all the time. If you want to change your wife, you'd better do that now, too, before you get quite old enough to be the father of the young girls to whom you find yourself attracted.

Sex is part of it. Men reach the peak of their sexual prowess at about eighteen, and it's downhill — although very gradually downhill — from there on. If you find, to your horror, that your performance in that field is not what it once was, you may be tempted to put the blame on your partner, to look for your own lost youth in the arms of a very young woman.

Athletic ability is part of it. Your tennis game is not as swift as it used to be. The ski slopes are steeper than they were ten years ago. You would rather watch a golf match on television than engage in one at the club. Perhaps your favorite belt seems to be shrinking a little. You are distressed in general by various little signs of physical deterioration.

Your job is part of the crisis, too. By this time you can tell pretty accurately how much final success you are going to achieve in your chosen career. If your job could be described more as a living than a career, you know that what you're doing right now is what you'll be doing until you retire, assuming that the company doesn't go bankrupt or get taken over by a giant conglomerate, in which case you may get fired. Both those prospects — staying in your present job or losing it — can look pretty bleak.

Oddly enough, if you have been very successful in your chosen career, you may find yourself even more miserable than somebody who is just getting by. You are exactly where you hoped, twenty years ago, that you would be. How come your position hasn't brought you the satisfactions you were sure would go with success?

Your sense of power over other people, whether at work or in your family circle, comes into play during a mid-life crisis. If you have always made most of the decisions in the family, you watch your children growing up, and you may find yourself becoming more controlling than ever, because you are afraid of the time, which suddenly seems frighteningly close, when they will be fully grown and making their own decisions. At work, you may see younger men getting more rapid promotions than you do.

Then there is a perhaps unconscious fear of your own death. Death, when you are in your twenties, is something that happens to other people. Death, when you are in your forties, may not seem exactly around the corner, but you can't help noticing that people in their forties turn up now and then in the obituary columns. Death, in other words, is not around *this* corner, but . . . three curves down the road?

This poem was written around 600 B.C. by Solon, the social reformer who transformed Athens into a democracy (he's the same fellow whose name is invoked in newspaper headlines such as, "Critic Accuses Solons of Gerrymandering District.") He divides a man's normal lifespan into ten periods of seven years each. The translation is by Karen Peterson.

The young child, not yet a man, grows and loses
his first teeth in the first seven years.
And when god has brought to an end the next seven
years,
he presents the body of a growing youth.
In the third, his limbs are still growing but
his chin grows downy, the flower of his changing
countenance.
In the fourth seven each man is outstanding in his
strength;
it is when men have excellent bodies.
In the fifth it is time for a man to be mindful of
marriage
and to seek children as descendants.
In the sixth the mind of a man is trained in all things,
and he does not still wish equally to do reckless deeds.
In the seventh seven he is by far best in mind and
speech,
as he is in the eighth, for a total of fourteen years.
In the ninth, he is still able, but his
speech and wisdom are losing their excellence.
And if one should come to the full measure having
finished the tenth,
he would not be unready to have the fate of death.
(Solon himself lived to be about eighty.)

Now, you will notice that Solon's sixth period, ages thirty-five to forty-two, is characterized by some loss of physical vigor, with a compensatory gain in mental ability. Solon's man could no longer compete physically with younger men, nor did he want to. He was moving on to another phase of his life.

You can, too.

Mid-Life Crisis in Women

For several reasons, mid-life crisis for women usually comes somewhat earlier than for men. One reason involves human biology and the child-bearing years. If you are a woman and you want a child, you know by the time you are thirty or thirty-five that your deadline is approaching with terrifying speed. You no longer have ten or fifteen years to make up your mind — with each passing year you become less fertile, and also more likely to bear an abnormal child. That's one kind of female mid-life crisis.

Another kind is almost the opposite. Suppose you are thirty-five, married, and have all the children you want? If you are typical, you have just sent your youngest off to school, and are now contemplating how best you can get back into the world of paid work. It isn't going to be easy. Only 30% of women aged thirty-five to forty-five have college degrees, and even that lucky 30% don't have it made. Their average salary is the same as that of a male high school dropout.

Sex, at this time of your life, may also rear its ugly head. Male sexuality, as we mentioned earlier, peaks at about eighteen. Female sexuality peaks at about thirty-eight. This does seem rather unfair of nature, but that's the way it is. It is probably impractical to go around looking for adolescent boys to seduce, but you may find yourself strongly tempted to feed your husband all known or rumored aphrodisiacs for

237

dinner, and if that doesn't produce any improvement, to embark on an affair with somebody else. Try to resist. Things will get better later on. If your husband is a few years older than you are, he's probably going through his own mid-life crisis while you're going through yours, and you're going for the moment in opposite directions: he's feeling he is stuck with the *status quo*, and you are feeling that it's about time you got to try *your* wings. If you care about your husband, hang in there; before you know it, you'll both be back on the same track.

How to Cope

A mid-life crisis is stressful. Stress is painful, but it is also a means of psychological growth. When you come to think about it, what aspects of your life cause the greatest stress? Probably your spouse, your children, your job, and your finances. And what aspects give you the greatest satisfaction from time to time? Probably your spouse, your children, your job, and your finances (although that last, we admit, is getting less likely all the time).

Mid-life crisis is like adolescence in that it is a time of great stress and it should also be a time of great growth. It is a time of transition. While you're going through it, you feel terrible, and you probably make everybody around you feel terrible, too. We understand and expect this when it comes to dealing with adolescent youngsters, but we have to come to believe that people's personalities are stabilized by the time they are twenty or so, and we are simply upset by any radical change in someone we love. If you are going around saying sadly to yourself, "Is this all there is to life? Somehow, I expected much more," your attitude is obviously going to affect your spouse and your children. Either they are going to feel they have failed

238

you, or they are going to get defensive and get angry with you; both natural reactions, but not pleasant either for you or for them.

Try to remember that you are going through a *transitional* period; in some ways, you may be reliving your adolescence. Just don't carry things to extremes. That is, if you are toying with the idea of having an affair with somebody, consider what would happen if it were discovered. What effect would it have on your marriage? your children? your career?

If you are thinking about changing jobs, do a little planning before you stamp in and tell your supervisor what you have *really* thought of him all these years.

Maybe raising sheep in Australia is the ideal way to spend your golden years. On the other hand, maybe you should do a little more research before you decide.

Do not, in other words, take any drastic steps until you are certain that your new desires are more than a passing fancy. You might make a list of the ten most stressful aspects of your life, and figure out which of them are under your control. Fix them as best you can, and see if you can live with the rest.

Before you fracture a relationship, be sure you know it is necessary to your happiness to do so. If you are a person of integrity, if honesty and responsibility are a part of your self-image, you owe it to yourself as well as to your spouse to consider long and hard whether a divorce is necessary. If your marriage has no emotional or physical intimacy, and this has been going on for a long time, perhaps you should get out. If it is a relatively recent drawing apart, you probably should not. You, as a person who values integrity, will value yourself less if you violate that integrity, if you act against your own long-held principles. You alone can decide the weight of the gains and losses which a divorce and perhaps a new relationship would bring. If you do get a divorce, will you spend the rest of your life liking yourself less than you used to do? feeling guilty about the unhappiness you have caused your family? Are you really sure that this is your last, best chance for a little happiness of your own?

Do you need help?

If you and your spouse have a good, intimate relationship, you can probably help each other. Talk about your feelings, even though this is likely to be hard at first, especially if you are a man. All too many men in our society simply don't know how to express their feelings, or even how to recognize their own feelings.

If you are a man, a mid-life crisis may be your opportunity to change this. Earning money is not all there is to life, and it may be that the empty, static feeling you are experiencing right now is your psyche trying to tell you something. Your abilities as a breadwinner are important to your family. So are your qualities as lover, husband, father; and in the long run it is from these last that your own greatest satisfactions will come, if you once learn how to share your feelings and be receptive to the feelings of your family.

If you are a woman, you probably are better at sharing your feelings, but you may need your self-confidence bolstered. You have spent years being responsive to your husband and your children. Now you want to be something besides somebody's wife and somebody's mother. If your family is not supportive, talk to a professional — a career counselor, a psychologist, a minister. And for goodness sake, if it's your husband who is going through a crisis, get him into therapy if you possibly can. Men are far more likely to act out their fantasies than women are. While you are still brooding about whether ten years of teaching small children to tie their shoelaces and count to a hundred could be converted into a marketable skill, your husband may be zipping down to the bank to convert your joint savings account into a Pacific cruise — with or without you, depending upon just how his fantasies go.

He feels that he is stuck in a bad place in his life, that the best years of his life are over, and that his life is meaningless, and he is thrashing desperately around to try to find a way out. Now, you may be pretty sure that those feelings are going to be temporary, but you probably won't be able to convince him of that. He needs to be able to express his fantasies in a safe place, to someone who will give him unconditional positive regard. It's going to be a little difficult for you to feel unconditional positive regard for the man who is trying to wreck your life. That's what therapists are for.

With or without professional help, it is possible for a marriage in which one or both of the partners went through a mid-life crisis to come out, not only intact, but closer and richer than it was before. Unfortunately, there is greater pressure in our society today to get divorced than there is to stay married. Our society is accustomed to a quick fix for any problem; if you only go around once, you deserve to be happy, and if you aren't happy, you owe it to yourself to get happy. It may seem that the obvious way to accomplish that is to leave your present life and forge a new one.

We disagree. We feel that if your marriage has any good features at all, it behooves both of you (even though one of you seems to be temporarily insane) to try to work things out with each other. You have a responsibility, not only to yourself, but to your partner and your children. Responsibility is not the same thing as self-sacrifice, however; there certainly are situations in which splitting up may be the only reasonable thing to do. Our concern is that divorce, rather than a last resort, is becoming the first thing people think about during a mid-life crisis.

A therapist can be very helpful; a non-judgmental outsider who is trained in psychology can help you to clarify your values, your feelings, and your frustrations at a much more rapid pace than you may be able to do it by yourselves. A therapist can show you, not how to ignore your fantasies or give them up, but how to convert them into realistic dreams which might become reality.

However you decide to handle the issue of mid-life crisis, do handle it somehow; don't just pretend it isn't happening. Confront it, work through it, and emerge happily on the other side. You have temporarily lost your perspective, but you'll find it — not the same one, but a better one — again.

And don't lose sight of the phrase which probably preserved your sanity when your children wanted to take a security blanket to school, or refused to eat any green vegetables, or lost a pair of glasses three times in one week, or started taking a minimum of three showers a day; "Don't worry; it's just a phase!"

Putting the Pieces Together

Putting the Pieces Together
(Continuity)

Have you ever worked one of those gigantic jigsaw puzzles — the kind you lay out on the pingpong table and fool with for weeks? Let's suppose you have a box with 1500 pieces. Assembled, they are supposed to give you a reproduction of a Breughel painting. And let us further suppose that you painstakingly put it all together, until you run out of pieces — and discover that you have half a dozen little gaps. Your box contained only 1494 pieces.

The general picture is clear, of course; there is a castle in the background, and the grassy clearing in the foreground is full of little medieval people going about their various occupations: making armor, making soup, making war, making love.

But what is causing that ominous shadow on the left turret of the castle? Can that leg really belong to the man with the bow? If not, what in the world is the owner of the leg doing? Is that a cockfight, a group of men bending over an injured companion — or what? You'll never know unless you see the original — your version has holes in it.

Life (to employ one of our many vivid similes) is something like that jigsaw puzzle. Where you will be in the future depends upon where you are now, and that in turn is dependent upon where you were in the past. Your sense of identity depends upon your feeling of continuity, of connection to the past and so to the future.

Just as your sense of continuity was outraged when you finished the puzzle as best you could, only to find those gaps — so your sense of continuity in real life may be warped by changes in your career, your friendships, your marriage, or many other connections.

A sense of identity is not a static concept; it is a process which continues all your life. You are — and you are more than — the little girl who collected shells or the little boy who was afraid of the dark. Even though you may not spend much time reminiscing about your remote past, all that you have experienced, all the choices you have made, go together to make up the individual, unique, irreplaceable person you are.

It is important to take stock of your life now and then, to make a sort of mental inventory; you must value each of your experiences, pleasant or unpleasant, and see where they fit in the whole picture.

The unexamined life (does this sound familiar?) is not worth living. Your sense of continuity leads to a sense of identity; this gives you a feeling of consistency, and it is that consistency of action which forms integrity.

Personal continuity

Your individual sense of continuity can be, if not shattered, at least somewhat fractured or strained whenever you make a major change in your life. This is not to say that you should never make major changes in your life, needless to say. But you should take time now and then to reflect on what you have done, to consider what you are about to do, and to be sure that your choices are the best ones that you can make, at the moment.

Nobody in the world makes all the right choices, but

if you spend time reflecting on your previous ones before you go on to new ones, you are going to improve your chances remarkably.

Most of us, unfortunately, do not spend enough time contemplating our own past. The idea, remember, is to *contemplate* — not to keep reliving, guilt, anger, grief or any other unpleasant emotion; but to remember, at this relatively safe distance, which of our choices turned out to be good ones, and to fit all of our experiences, good and bad, into our present identity.

Friendships

Do you still keep in touch with some of the people you knew in college, in high school, even in elementary school? Even though you have probably grown in different directions and may well have little in common, it does give you a sort of warm, reassuring feeling, doesn't it, to have someone say, "Do you remember the time you and Jerry and I were fooling around the old water tower, and he fell from halfway up, and we were sure he was dead — but he only had the wind knocked out of him? As long as I live, I don't think I'll ever forget how I felt right then."

You and your friend might not like each other if you met for the first time today, but for the moment, that doesn't matter much; that shared memory gives you both a deep feeling of continuity.

You have to keep a sense of perspective about old friendships, however. While they are valuable in enhancing continuity, they may also be hampering to' both of you. You keep changing throughout life, and so does your friend. The reasons you were friends as children had to do with the needs you each had then; if your needs have changed, you do not have to keep bowling together every second Thursday. Just reflect a bit before you jettison any part of your past.

Career

Whenever you change jobs, your sense of continuity is threatened, and the more radical the change, the more you are jeopardizing your sense of continuity, and, therefore, your sense of identity. Moving from one company to another while doing similar work is not usually a major dislocation in a career sense (although if you are moving to another city, where you will have to build new friendships, *that* part of your identity will be threatened).

Moving from one field to another is much more serious. When you start a really new career, you are likely to feel some anxiety, no matter how exciting and rewarding you think the new job is likely to be. Until you have really become accustomed to it — have achieved a sense of mastery over it — your sense of self is on the line: you have exchanged something known for something unknown, and your sense of continuity has been disrupted.

Marriage

One of the joys of a long-term marriage is the accumulation of shared memories. The time you went camping together and woke to find seventeen cows all leaning on the fence, solemnly chewing their cuds and staring at your tent. The time the station wagon didn't have enough power to get quite to the top of a pass, and you had to back down for half a mile of corkscrew curves before you could turn around. The time you went to listen to a famous jazz pianist and he refused to play anything but "Tea for Two" all evening.

Nothing dramatic, nothing earthshaking — just fun to remember together.

The longer you have been married, the more shared memories you have, the more the sense of continuity of each of you is bound up with the other. People used to assume, if a couple had been married for fifteen or twenty years, that they would stay together for the rest of their lives. This is not an assumption one can take for granted any more; but if you have been married for many years and are becoming estranged, you owe it to yourselves to be sure that your divorce is not a capricious one.

Get counselling, make sure you can't manage a reconciliation, try, in other words, to stay married to each other if the situation makes any sense at all. Because your own individual sense of continuity is intimately tied in with the mutual memories shared by you and your spouse. You may think all you will feel after your divorce is a sense of relief. You will really feel, whatever your other emotions, a sense of loss — a discontinuity. There, for better or for worse, goes a large part of your identity, in the person of your ex-spouse.

Family continuity

An important part of your self-definition comes from your family. This is why adopted children, when they have become adults, will often go to extraordinary lengths to see their natural parents — not necessarily to develop a closeness with them, but just to see them and talk to them; to get a sense of continuity.

Family continuity is important in both directions: children and grandchildren like the feeling that they have a family background, that they are part of a larger continuous process. It is reassuring to know that Aunt Lucy, who is now a physicist, also had problems with fractions when she was your age; and that you and Grandpa share a passion for walking in the woods in the very early morning.

Parents and grandparents, given a new baby in the

family, are given to saying things like, "I think she has her father's chin, don't you?" or "Have I ever showed you Emily's first picture? Little Debbie is the spittin' image of her at that age!"

The adult generations have to be careful about extrapolating resemblances too far: it isn't fair to a child to insist that she have the dancing career her mother gave up when she married, or that he enroll at the college that Grandpa had to drop out of when the Great Depression came along.

Talents, interests, aptitudes do run in families; but while little Debbie may turn out to look like Great Aunt Emily, to share some of her enthusiasms, to have some of her talents — little Debbie is *not* Great Aunt Emily. Debbie is her own individual, unique self. She is part of the continuity of her family, but she is more than just an extension of her ancestors, too; she is also herself, and she needs to develop her own balance of similarities and differences, as do we all.

Heirlooms

The oldest generation in a family ought to be the dispensors of memories, of wisdom — and of worldly goods.

If you are, say, a grandparent — please try not to bristle at that statement. We are *not* saying that you should divide up your estate now and live on an allowance from your grown children. We are talking about heirlooms — things that have been in your family long enough to have sentimental as well as monetary value.

To give is more blessed than to receive, in a very profound sense. Have you ever had as much pleasure from a present someone gave you, as you got when you gave the perfect present to someone else? When you went to six different stores, if you were shopping for your gift, or secreted yourself for hours in your work-shop, if you were making it — and wrapped it carefully, and handed it to your loved one, and waited breath-lessly for his or her reaction?

Just as it's more fun to give somebody a gift in person, rather than to mail it and wait for a note or a telephone call of acknowledgement — so it's more fun to give away your heirlooms while you are still around to enjoy the reaction. Again, we are not talking about the silver coffee service you use every time you have the bridge club over; we are talking about that cut glass vase in the attic, the gold watch that your grandfather brought over from Germany, the copper teapot from Sweden.

Pick your recipients with care. Which of your children or grandchildren would really treasure the rocking chair, the locket, the model ship? Don't just guess — talk to them about it.

Both John and Jeanne's relatives have been very discerning in this respect. John's father, for instance, went to the Massachusetts Institute of Technology, and while there, he bought a slide rule: a Polyphase Duplex slide rule, made by Keuffel-Essen. These slide rules were imported from Germany beginning in 1883, made in this country beginning in 1891 — and now you can't buy them anywhere. They haven't been made since 1972. John's son Chris plans to be an engineer, and when his grandfather gave him the slide rule — well, a more perfect present would be hard to find. It has become a part of Chris' sense of identity.

John's father also made a beautiful, elaborate family tree. John treasures it, and his children are fascinated by it.

Jeanne's mother-in-law, over the years, has given a number of heirlooms to the younger members of the family, and whenever any of the group is visiting her, she tries to find out who would really appreciate a given item most. She has no plans to strip herself of things she treasures and enjoys using just yet — but she has a very good idea of who would like what when the time comes.

Some years ago, when Jeanne's children were about ten, eight, and six, the eight-year-old suddenly said, "Mommie, when you die, can I have your books?" "I would like Daddy's records," chimed in the youngest; and "I want that blue vase," said the oldest.

After her first shocked reaction (well, what a bunch of little ghouls *you* three turned out to be!) Jeanne realized that this was becoming a very useful conversation: she was finding out not only what things each child treasured particularly, but why. (Alan wanted the records because he liked sets of things; he wanted the encyclopedias for the same reason). It's a conversation that has been repeated, with variations, over the years since then.

It is a lot easier to discuss this sort of thing when death, so far as you know, is not imminent. Easier on you, and easier on the kids. But you do have to keep asking at intervals — that shotgun collection so admired by the ten-year-old may be more valued by somebody else in the family when twenty years have gone by.

Making a will

Far too many people put this off. Some have a sort of superstitious feeling that writing a will is akin to signing their own death warrant — once they've done it, death will come and get them. Others feel that their estate is so small that it's not worth bothering about.

If you have any assets at all, and anyone in the world you care about — you ought to have a will.

Harney's best friend at college shared his passion for early jazz records. When they both joined the service, each made a will leaving his collection to his friend. They both survived, married, had children, and of course changed their wills. But just having made those wills proved to be very comforting to each of them. It's enough of a worry dodging snipers' bullets without also contemplating your invaluable record collection being carted off to Goodwill if you aren't, in the end, an artful enough dodger.

Jeanne and Harney made their first joint will when they took an automobile trip to the west coast, leaving their two preschoolers in the care of friends in Denver. They were in their twenties and perfectly healthy — it was the thought of those crazy California drivers that got to them. A will, in short, gives you a certain amount of peace of mind, whether you are setting up guardians for your children in case of an eventuality which you trust will not come to pass — which is unlikely to come to pass — but just might, or whether you are simply making sure that your Complete Works of Agatha Christie pass into appreciative hands.

We are all going to die some day. Accidents do happen. Fatal diseases strike people of any age.

Make a will. Make it fair. And consult your heirs as to what they really value. If you are leaving money split among several children or grandchildren — the split should be equitable. Not necessarily even — just equitable. And if you are cutting someone out, or down, you ought to explain why — either in person or in your will. It isn't fair to expect a gaggle of grown children, and their spouses, and their children, to decide among themselves what is fair. That's your job — and then you can have the added satisfaction of knowing that your heirs are getting what you want them to have.

That's a form of continuity which extends even beyond the grave.

Why is continuity important?

In a sense, we are all getting ready for death.

Whether our age, our health, our circumstances indicate that we have another half century or another ten days, it behooves us to take time to reflect, now and then, upon our past life.

Think about the choices you have made: have they been mostly good, or mostly bad? Or do you feel you have seldom made deliberate choices — have circumstances simply carried you along? All of us have had dreams; all of us, probably, have fallen short of the mark. Don't despair if your mental inventory tells you that you've made more than your share of bad choices. Part of the human condition is a certain degree of imperfection. Everyone has impacted other lives perhaps more strongly than he or she knows — sometimes for good, sometimes for bad. That's just the way life is. However, every human being is also a person of worth. Appreciate that, and whatever your age, whatever your hopes or fears for the future, pause every now and then and reap the harvest of whatever it is that you have done thus far.

A sense of continuity in one's life leads to a sense of identity; and a strong sense of identity leads to consistent action and a firm sense of values. You can work this in both directions, in a way — your consistent actions, the kinds of choices you tend to make, indicate what your real values are; and your values influence the choices you make.

You could set these ideas up in a kind of imperfect equation: Continuity (Identity + Integrity + Values) = Wisdom.

The equation is imperfect because the total, Wisdom,

is really greater than the sum of its parts. Many of us have at least a degree of integrity; many have a sense of identity; many have firm values. But unless you have all of them — you don't have wisdom.

And few of us are wise even now and then; while nobody who is human is wise at all times.

Keep your perspective and do the best you can with what you have right now, what you have had in the past, what you may have in the future.

And so will we.

The Best is Yet to Be — Maybe!

The Best is Yet to Be — Maybe!

(Old Age)

Grow old along with me
The best is yet to be—
The last of life, for which the first was made:
Any young or middle-aged American reading
Browning's verse today is likely to respond with a
heartfelt, "Oh, yeah?"

Conventional wisdom has it that America is a
terrible place in which to grow old.

If you read the newspapers, you know that once you
pass 65 (or maybe even 50) shoddy repairmen are going
to talk you into unnecessary furnace replacements and
roof repairs. Itinerant con artists are going to pose as
bank inspectors and winkle your life savings out of
you. As you totter down the street to deposit your Social
Security check, some young punk is going to mug you.

If you watch television commercials, you realize that
you are going to be stricken with arthritis, heartburn,
hemorrhoids, constipation, and the heartbreak of
psoriasis, not to mention having problems with
dentures, fallen arches, falling hair, and tired blood.

Your grown children will ignore you, your fixed
income will not be able to keep up with inflation, and
finally you will wind up in a nursing home, where
callous aides will abuse you and the manager will try
his best to divert your meagre funds into his private
bank account.

It is quite true, of course, that some of these things

257

happen to some older people. It is also true that horror stories make the news because they are unusual — some old people are indeed neglected or even abused. So are some children. Neither is the norm.

Most older Americans seem to be doing very well, enjoying life and coping with their problems about as well as they used to when they were younger.

Part of the difficulty in thinking about old age is a matter of perception, of point of view. If you are seventeen and into motorcycles and discos, you may well believe that life when you have to walk with a cane will not be worth living. Wait fifty years; if you have been maturing as well as getting older, it's likely that motorcycles and discos will bore you stiff.

Jeanne's daughter Susan did some illuminating research once for a sociology class. She interviewed a handful of retired people who lived in their own homes in a Denver suburb, she talked to a collection of old people who shared a group home, and she visited three or four nursing homes and discussed life with the people there.

The people who lived in their own homes were enjoying it. Their incomes were smaller than they had been, but since they were no longer buying shoes and peanut butter for little kids or paying college tuition for older kids or buying major appliances (they already had all the furniture and appliances they wanted), and their mortgages had long since been paid off, their reduced income was enough. Even with inflation, they had more discretionary income than they had ever had. They were all quite happy, involved in church or civic affairs, pursuing hobbies (some of which were money-makers as well), and socializing more than they had when they were younger and under pressure to work hard, get ahead, raise children, and acquire material things.

"But of course," they said, "I'm happy because I'm in good health and able to live in my own home. I would *hate* to live in a nursing home!"

The group home had about eight elderly people who shared facilities. The one who could drive took those who could not shopping or to appointments; those who could cook did so, and others took care of the garden or cleaned the house. These people were happy, too. They teased each other, but they supported each other, too. They had each been alone before this experiment in group living, and all felt that they were better off now, having companionship and help with the necessary chores.

"The people I feel sorry for," they said, "are the ones who are all alone, children grown up and moved away, and nobody to talk to. I used to live like that, and I would *hate* to do it again!"

Interestingly enough, the nursing home patients were happy, too. They were all more handicapped than the other two groups; that's why they were in a nursing home. But they were all able to get around to an extent, and those who were most mobile would go down the hall to visit those who were less so.

One of the nursing homes was in a very quiet suburban setting. The people who lived there had chosen it for that reason, and they all mentioned appreciatively that they no longer had to listen to the rock music or the motorcycle repair work which had been constantly going on in the places where they had lived; they definitely did not want to be in a community of mixed ages.

Another nursing home was in Denver, a high-rise located on a busy street. The people who chose this one did so because they wanted to be where the action was.

They could walk down the street to a dry cleaner, a drug store, a movie, or a restaurant, and they could look out of their windows and see what was going on.

With the nursing homes — all of them — the main complaint was the food. "Well," one woman said philosophically, "it's about like the food I had when I was in college. They do their best, poor things, but let's face it — institutional cooking just never is as good as you can do at home. On the other hand, I don't have to wash the dishes. It certainly could be worse."

This research of Susan's was not scientifically valid, of course; she just worked out a questionnaire and went around chatting with people she knew or with those in the group home and nursing homes who were willing to talk to her. Those people were the most gregarious and perhaps the most physically healthy. On the other hand, it's thought-provoking, isn't it, that she didn't run across one person who was miserable?

A more scientific survey was done a few years ago in a lower middle class section of Chicago. The people included were all elderly widows, and all lived alone in small apartments. The sociologists expected to find loneliness, bitterness, fear, and straitened circumstances. Well, the circumstances were straitened, all right, but the ladies were cheerful. They had worked hard all their lives, most had raised large families, and now they were enjoying the bliss of living all by themselves, accountable to nobody. They walked to nearby grocery stores when they felt like it, and they took a bus downtown when they felt like that. No more breakfasts to fix, no more lunches to pack, no more clothes to wash and mend and iron. Nobody else tracking mud in, nobody saying, "You gonna stay up all night finishing that dumb magazine?" The major emotion these women exhibited when talking about their dead husbands and their moved-away children was — relief. The average woman in this group had a visit from one of her children about once every six months — and seemed to feel that was plenty — perhaps more than enough. What these women were enjoying was freedom. For the first time in their lives, they could please themselves rather than their families.

Then there was the woman who entered a nursing home when she was in her seventies, not because she needed nursing services, but because her husband did. He had had a stroke, and she didn't want to be parted from him. For ten years, she took care of him devotedly; she was the only one who could interpret his speech. He died, and the staff expected her to die, too — he had in essence been her whole life for so long, they were afraid that she would grieve herself into a grave. She did mourn him — for about a month. You see, for ten years he had not been the man she married — she loved him, yes, but really she had lost him long ago, and she had done most of her grieving then.

After that month, she pulled herself together and became the terror of the nursing home staff. She took notes on the quality and quantity of food and shot off memos to the cooks; she ran her finger along the window sills and berated the cleaning people; she put together a grievance committee of patients who had complaints about service, and got action. Ten years have passed, and she's still going strong. Now that she's got the nursing home shaped up, she's meddling in local politics, and everybody who knows her is confident that the piece of parkland behind the nursing home is *not* going to be rezoned to provide another shopping center.

How about the inevitable infirmities of old age? Isn't

it true that your reflexes slow, your strength wanes, your memory becomes unreliable, and your learning ability decreases? Yes and no.

As you age, your reflexes do indeed become slower and your strength and stamina are not what they were at twenty. However, if you have watched Marlin Perkins roping zebras or Jacques Cousteau bringing up bits of debris from the bottom of the Mediterranean, you can see that this loss is relative: those two have been physically active all their lives, and they still are.

Arturo Toscanini, Pablo Casals, and Georgia O'Keeffe had talents which developed early on, and they kept right on using them and improving their skills. Grandma Moses, on the other hand, discovered her painting talent late in life, and Edith Hamilton, who had a long and distinguished career as a scholar and teacher, wrote her first book when she was in her sixties, and followed it up with several more, all highly successful.

There are many people who are climbing mountains, skiing, and running cross country races at advanced ages. More typically, however, people do find they tire more easily and they move more slowly. So what? Some of the most enjoyable occupations don't require much in the way of strength, stamina, or speed.

As far as intellectual skills are concerned, most older people can learn as well as younger ones. If you want to learn a foreign language, a new skill, or a new concept at eighty, go right ahead, and don't let anybody tell you that learning is for kids. You have all those years of learning behind you, and the more you already know, the easier it is to add things to your store of knowledge. All those eager little synapses have more potential connections to make.

Of course, if you are the sort of person who stopped

reading — or thinking — when you finished high school, it will be harder for you to learn things when you're old. That's a choice you should have made, ideally, when you were relatively young, but if you didn't, don't despair; it may take you a little longer to get into the study habits you dropped a few decades ago, but if you want to do it, you can.

Reading is great mental exercise. If you're young, start now; you might be surprised at the difference between a book and its motion picture or TV adaptation. If you're old, we don't have to tell you this — you already know how to read.

Remember that old age, even more than beauty, is in the eye of the beholder. When you were fifteen, thirty seemed pretty well over the hill, even if you were not of the generation determined never to trust anyone over thirty. Remember, too, that aging is a continuous process, and that many of life's less pleasant experiences — the first gray hair, the first bifocals, menopause — happen to most of us when we are middle-aged rather than really old.

Jeanne once visited her father and a group of his contemporaries. One of them said, "I do hope I never live to be old." Since all those present except Jeanne were in their mid-seventies, this seemed a rather odd statement, until she learned that one woman had recently buried a 103-year-old parent, and another had a 98-year-old father whose arthritis had become worse in the last year.

With the American emphasis on youth, it's a compliment to say, "How do you stay so young?"

It shouldn't be.

Old age has accumulated wisdom, experience, and humor which younger people could well envy. We as a culture are losing a great deal by looking at people *as we think they are* rather than as they really are, individuals who are probably more different from each other than are younger people. The longer you live, the more different from anybody else you become; you can't talk about "What do senior citizens want?" any more sensibly than you can talk about "What do thirty-year-olds want?" With either group, it all depends. Some old people want conviviality, others appreciate solitude. Some want to keep physically active, others want to keep mentally active, and still others appreciate the chance to slow down, to rest, to stop keeping score.

It seems to us that the most important factor in a happy old age is a sense of self-worth. Most people past middle age find themselves reevaluating their lives, considering their accomplishments and their failures, putting things in perspective.

In one way or another, you have, by the time you're seventy or eighty or ninety, affected a lot of lives. If you can look back and feel that more often than not, you have changed those lives for the better — or at least not changed them for the worse — you have a right to be proud of yourself.

We're going to tell you about the four elderly people we know and love best: John's mother and father, and Jeanne's mother-in-law and father. Each of them is a unique individual and an interesting person; each of them has found a different — and successful — way of coping with advancing age.

There is an ancient Chinese curse: "May you live in interesting times." Anybody who is now in their seventh or eighth decade has indeed lived through interesting times. Some of them were old enough to serve in World War I; they all lived through the Great Depression and World War II and Korea and inflation, scarcities and gluts. Just surviving those times is something to be proud of; people who have had successful, useful lives deserve a great deal more credit than society usually gives them.

Take John's mother, for example. She used to write for magazines, but she devoted herself for years to keeping her husband and her three sons happy. She was, in the best sense of the word, a professional mother; she was selfless in putting other people's needs ahead of her own. She is a spontaneous, feeling kind of person with an infectious personality, and it was her caring and her optimism that helped all her sons through the inevitable emotional crises that go along with growing up.

She played jazz piano, and when the boys were in high school it was her enthusiasm that led to their learning to play jazz. They all still do, and it's an important part of all their lives. She is still intensely interested in her family, and a most useful critic. She kept in touch with John's development of his game, "Gone Bananas," and we've been sending her this book chapter by chapter and paying close attention to her comments.

John's father retired in his fifties, and has been busier after that than he had ever been before. He was a successful businessman, and still keeps active with stock market and real estate investments. He likes to hunt and fish, play golf, read, paint (he has done many excellent watercolors, some of them commissioned), and garden.

John's father set an example of high standards for his family, because he set high standards for himself. That sense of excellence does not depend on competing with other people so much as competing with his own past performance; his own sense of autonomy has helped his sons develop theirs.

Jeanne's father is eighty-two. He was married to Jeanne's mother until she died, after twenty-eight happy years. Most of those years were Depression years; he worked and worried, they both stinted themselves to provide for three children, and they made it. She was the one who did the day to day disciplining; he was the one who set the standards for the family. Never once did any of the kids try to ride a bus for half fare after they turned twelve; never once did any of them keep the wrong change at a checkout stand. They didn't cheat on school exams then, and they don't cheat on their income tax now.

Then he married again, and had another long and happy marriage, until his second wife, too, died. Now he's seeing a lot of another very nice woman. They don't plan to marry, since they both value their privacy (and their pension plans), but they spend a lot of time together. Growing old does not have to mean growing lonely, or foregoing intimacy.

Jeanne's mother-in-law, who is now eighty-seven, was a teacher before she married. She is active in church affairs, on the local library board, interested in school activities. She belongs to a study club which has met once a month for about half a century, contributing her share (and more) of programs. For years she led a group of Campfire Girls. She is the local authority on birds.

Last summer she took a course in creative writing, during which she wrote her autobiography (she parlayed that into a couple of programs, one for study club and one for PEO). Now she is completing a history of her town, as coauthor of a book requested by the history museum, in which she is, of course, also active. In her spare time, she tutors illiterate adults.

The point about this delightful woman is that she has always been active. She has had trouble for years, ever since she began to look a bit like a little old lady, with people offering her rides, when she simply wants to walk around the countryside and look at birds. People — younger people who have, so to speak, grown up in cars — seem unable to comprehend that there are those who walk for pleasure.

This summer she said, "This past two years has been one of the most exciting periods in my whole life." You don't have to spend your later years reminiscing about the happier times you had in your youth. Sometimes you can live your happiest times in old age.

Now this has been a very upbeat chapter, hasn't it? We know that many older people have problems — problems with money, health, isolation, a feeling of uselessness. We feel it's important to you to realize two things about aging: first, you, when you are old, will be basically what you are now. Are you selfish, dogmatic, unwilling to take advice? You'll be even more so when you're eighty. Are you warm, generous, loving? Open to new ideas? Interested in your family, your friends, and the world in general? So will you be when you are old.

Second, we believe society is far too skewed in favor of youth. If we write off everybody over 65, we will lose the cream of our talent, our maturity, our accumulated wisdom. Childhood and adolescence are times of self-centeredness, confusion, fumbling for the right decisions, groping for maturity. Very few people in their twenties and thirties know themselves as well as they will a decade — or two or three decades — later. Everybody has to begin by growing up; only then can you grow wise. We as a society cannot afford to lose that wisdom.

Let me grow lovely, growing old—
So many fine things do.
Laces, and ivory, and gold
And silks need not be new;
And there is healing in old trees,
Old streets a glamour hold;
Why may not I, as well as these,
Grow lovely, growing old?

—Karle Wilson Baker

Getting Your Act Together

Getting Your Act Together

(Therapy)

The chapters in this book are all self-contained — except this one. If you have not yet read the chapter on communication (Why Don't You Listen to What I'm Trying to Say?), you'd better do it before you read this one.

That chapter had four people going on a picnic. The time is now five years later, and the same people are once again getting together for an outing.

"Well," says Sandra, screwing the lid on a thermos bottle, "do you think that's it?"

Theo looks at his checklist. "Everything except the fishing gear. Do you want me to get that?"

"Thanks, Theo. I'll go and put some lipstick on before the Sanfords get here."

Ingrid and Felix turn up right on time. Felix carries a package of steaks, and Ingrid carries a small sketch book and a large chocolate cake.

"Ingrid, that looks marvelous," says Sandra. "Did you make that yourself?"

Ingrid says complacently, "Yes, indeed. When Felix started spending practically every evening taking classes, I had to find something to do with my time, so I took some classes in gourmet cooking. Actually, I do most of the cooking now."

"I'll bet Felix still does most of the dusting," Sandra comments. "I'm sorry, Ingrid, I didn't mean to say that, it just sort of popped out."

Theo and Felix speak almost in unison: "Why don't we get started?"

Theo drives this time. Ingrid pouts a little, but the other three carry on a cheerful conversation. Ingrid wants to stop to make a sketch, but is overruled by the others on the basis that the sky up ahead looks a little cloudy, and they want to get everything set up before a shower arrives. Theo chooses the picnic site, and everybody scatters to look for firewood. Ingrid comes back with one small piece of wood and three attractive rocks, but the rest have found enough for a good fire, and soon steaks and sweet corn are cooking merrily away. The food is ready just in time; the foursome finishes the cake in the car as the rain begins.

"Know what, Sandra?" Theo asks cheerfully. "I forgot to bring any raingear."

"Oh, well," says Sandra with equal good humor, "it's going to clear in a minute or two anyway. That timing was great, wasn't it? Ingrid, this cake tastes even better than it looks. Is it a secret, or can I have your recipe?"

Ingrid has been staring moodily out the window. Suddenly she flings herself out of the car and rushes over to a nearby tree. "Why didn't somebody tell me I'd left my sketchbook here?" she wails. "It's soaking wet, it'll never be the same, what shall I do?"

The rain has now stopped, and everybody gets out of the car bearing paper napkins and sympathy. "Maybe if you blot it very gently, and keep turning the pages as they dry, you can save most of it," says Felix. "Tell you what, Ingrid, it's our turn to clean up. We'll keep turning pages while we do it, and Theo and Sandra can go fishing."

"How can you ask me to do something like cleaning pots when my last six weeks' work is lying in ruins before my very eyes?" asks Ingrid.

"Ingrid," says Felix, "would you rather wash or dry?"

"Neither one, I told you."

"I'm sorry about the sketchbook, Ingrid, but I don't think it's completely ruined, and we do need to get at those dishes. Come on now, honey, let's get with it."

Ingrid does.

An hour later Sandra and Theo come back, hand in hand. Sandra has five fish, and Theo has none. "They were really biting," Sandra says jokingly. "Only Theo spent forty-five minutes deciding on what fly to use, and by that time I'd got all there were in the pool."

Theo laughs sheepishly. "I *am* getting better at making decisions, really. I just backslide sometimes. This was one of the times."

"You've changed a lot, Theo," says Sandra. "But then, so have I. It used to drive me up the wall when you would want to have *all* the facts before you decided anything. I remember when we bought the car — you spent weeks checking out prices and mileage and frequency of repair charts and — well, everything. But we've had it four years now, and it's never given us a bit of trouble. I really appreciate that kind of careful research now. Five years ago, I would have picked a car out the way I'd choose a sweater: the price seems OK and I like the color."

"That's true, Sandra," says Felix. "Theo's getting faster at making decisions, and you're beginning to take more time. Pretty soon you're going to meet each other in the middle."

"Speaking of changes," says Theo. "When do we start calling you *Doctor* Sanford, Felix?"

"About another month, if all goes well. I don't know why I didn't go to graduate school years ago. I forgot how much I really loved studying. I'll be glad to get my degree, of course, but I'm almost sorry to have it over. It's been one of the best periods of my whole life. But I'm looking forward to working at the Mental Health Clinic, too. A few years of experience there, and I should be able to set up my own practice, or go into partnership with somebody. You know, I used to love those encounter sessions — but now, to know that pretty soon I'll be getting *paid* to do something I'm good at, and that I love doing — well, it just feels great!"

"We've all changed a lot," says Ingrid thoughtfully.

Everybody looks at her in silence, and she grins impishly. "Well, maybe I haven't changed all that much. I guess I'm still a textbook case of the Only Child Syndrome. But at least now, I know it, and I do try to think of other people some of the time."

Sandra says, "I think you're right, Ingrid. You and I have never hit it off — different chemistry or something, I guess — but I do like you better than I used to. What I'm trying to say is, I've learned that I'm me and you're you, and we shouldn't expect each other to think alike, or act alike. I used to get impatient with anybody who wasn't pretty much like me — and you're *so* different from me —" She breaks off and giggles. "And I bet you're thinking 'Thank God for that!' "

"Five years ago," Ingrid retorts, "I wouldn't just have thought it — I'd have said it. See how much I've improved?"

This breaks everybody up, and they all drive cheerfully down the mountain.

It is clear that these people and their relationships with each other have changed a good deal. Felix no longer fights Ingrid's battles for her, and Ingrid has reluctantly learned that life entails responsibilities as

274

well as pleasures. Felix has turned his love of helping people into a paying profession, and has collected the necessary credentials to do it. Theo has become more decisive, and Sandra and he have both relaxed and come closer to each other; they can both find humor in situations which five years ago would have created only irritation. Sandra has abdicated from some parts of her former role; she still makes many of the decisions for her family, but if Theo wants to make one, she not only lets him, she encourages him.

What has happened to these people? Five years have passed — that's part of it. And they have all had therapy — that's by far the more important part.

Oddly enough, it was Theo who first decided to go into therapy. Of course, he was heartily encouraged by Felix. Two months after the first picnic, he turned up at the office of a psychologist, whom we might as well call Dr. H. John Lyke. Here are bits of their first interview:

Theo introduces himself and immediately catechizes John about his credentials: where did he get his graduate degrees, how long has he been in practice, what is his background? Satisfied about John's professional respectability, he sits back and waits for John to make the next move.

"Why are you here, Mr. Ferguson?" John asks.

"If you mean why am I here in your office, it's because a friend of mine, Felix Sanford, recommended you. He heard you give a lecture once, and he was impressed. I suppose I ought to tell you, you're the third — well, Felix runs these encounter groups, and I went to one of them, but I didn't like it. All these emotional people sitting around, telling each other things I wouldn't even tell myself, and crying and hugging each other and yelling at each other — well, I could see it wasn't for me. Then I went to see our company psychologist, but I didn't feel comfortable with her, either. I kept thinking, I know she's not supposed to talk about her clients, but after all, she's only human, and what if I say something that makes her think I'm — weird, or unstable, and it gets back to my department head? So I asked Felix, and he told me about you. If you mean why do I want to see *any* therapist, well, it all started at a picnic a couple of months ago . . ."

There are long pauses this first session, but John learns something about Theo's background.

"My father is an accountant. Been with the same firm since he finished college. First full time job he ever had — in fact, he worked summers for the same outfit while he was finishing his degree — and he never saw any reason to change. They suit him, and I guess he must suit them; he gets a small raise every year. My mother doesn't have an outside job, but the way she runs that house! All the time I was growing up, I never once asked her where something was that she couldn't put her finger on instantly. And talk about being a spotless housekeeper — my mother is one of those people about whom people say, "You could eat off her floors.""

John says, "You told me you are married. Would you like to tell me something about your wife?"

There is a *very* long pause.

Finally Theo says, "You're going to think this is a terrible thing to say about my own wife."

"Whatever you say, I'm not going to think it's terrible. I'm not here to judge you; I'm here to help you find out what's troubling you and whether you can change it."

"Well, that will make a nice change," Theo answers bitterly. "My wife, Sandra, is *always* judging me. I don't know how much longer I can put up with it, I really don't. She used to kid me about being indecisive, but lately it isn't kidding any more — it's more like nagging. It's as if she feels — I guess contempt is the word — for me. Now I know I take a long time to make up my mind, but she's always jumping to conclusions, and I don't think that's any better, do you?"

"Perhaps not. Tell me, how do you yourself feel about this? *Are* you indecisive, do you think?"

Theo says slowly, "Yes. Yes, I am. I suppose that's why I resent Sandra's comments so much, because I know she's right. You know, I told you that you were the third therapist I've gone to. Well, you're really the fifth. I went to two others and didn't like either of them. But I think I can feel comfortable talking to you. And I think now that my main problem is my inability to make decisions. If you can fix that, most of my problems with Sandra will be over."

"I don't have all the answers, and I can't fix anything about your personality. Why don't you plan to come in once a week, and we'll see how things go."

Theo kept coming back, and was enthusiastic about the sessions. Naturally, he talked to Felix, and after a couple of months Felix too made an appointment.

"You call me Felix, and I'll call you John, all right? I always find that in my encounter groups — I suppose Theo told you about my encounter groups? — anyway, I always find that getting on a first name basis right away makes people more relaxed. You know, you and I are really in the same line of business, aren't we? How about a professional discount?"

After inquiring into Felix's financial circumstances, John does agree to a discount — but not a professional discount.

"Last Tuesday night," says Felix, "was just the last straw. Now understand, I love my wife dearly. She's the most beautiful woman I ever saw, and even though we've been married ten years it's as though we're still on our honeymoon. And she's so talented . . . well, anyway, last Tuesday night I was tired. Ingrid was at her art class, and I had finished cleaning up the kitchen — she's so wrapped up in her painting she can't concentrate on doing things around the house, and I don't expect her to — but anyway, I was pretty tired by the time I sat down to do something about the bills. And there was a notice from the bank that both our accounts were overdrawn. Ingrid puts her salary into her own checking account and uses it for classes and art supplies and things like that, and she pays for her clothes out of our joint account. But she's never learned to balance a checkbook, and half the time she forgets to fill in the stub. We both earn pretty good money, and we really shouldn't have any trouble living within our income, but somehow — well, I just sat there thinking about my whole life. I'm going to be thirty next month, and I've been working for almost ten years, and here I can't pay my bills. I love doing those encounter sessions, but I do them as a volunteer. I'd hate to give them up, but I began feeling maybe I should take an evening job instead. Ingrid is out so much she probably wouldn't even notice I was gone."

It develops that Felix is the youngest of four children, and was very close to his mother while he was growing up. She felt unappreciated, and he was sympathetic. He became a good listener with a great deal of empathy for other people. He met Ingrid during their senior year at college, and the attraction was instant and mutual: he was enchanted by her good looks and her artistic talent, and she was enchanted by his open adoration of her.

"Your friend Theo told me about a picnic you had

together a few months ago," says John. "He seemed to feel it was a turning point for him. I'd like to get your impression of what happened."

"Theo told me he was embarrassed for Sandra — the way she lashed out at Ingrid — and so concerned about things that might go wrong that he didn't enjoy himself at all," says Felix. "I was concerned because Theo seemed so down, but all in all I had a good time. It was really pretty funny to see Sandra blow up like that; she's usually in pretty tight control of herself. Now if she'd just learn to go with the flow . . ."

Sandra was the next of the foursome to come and see John.

John mentions that she seems pretty tense, and asks if she would like a cup of tea.

"At a dollar a minute? No indeed. I want to get right down to business."

"Actually," says John, "it's a little more than a dollar a minute; I charge $60.00 for a fifty-minute session. All right, why have you come to see me?"

"Because I'm sure that Theo has been giving you some pretty strange accounts of me and our life together, and I thought it might be cheaper in the long run if I gave you the real facts. He tells me that you and he are working on his indecisiveness; and I would be truly grateful if you can really do something about that. Do you know that man comparison shops for handkerchiefs? I make practically all the decisions in our marriage, not because I like doing it, but because somebody has to do it, and Theo either can't or won't. I'm sure he resents it — he sort of lies in wait and pounces when one of my decisions is wrong. He's been interested in photography for a long time, and recently he's been spending so much time in the darkroom that I thought I'd try to help him. The truth is, I've been

279

lonely; we used to share things, but lately — well, anyway, I was mixing the chemicals for the developer, and I guess I read the directions too fast, because I got the proportions wrong and ruined the whole batch of pictures. Well, you would have thought the end of the world had come! They were just pictures of our back yard, and he went out and shot the same scenes the next day — but he got so mad at me he wouldn't speak to me for a week."

Sandra, it turns out, is the older of two children. Her father deserted her mother when Sandra was three, and her little brother was a few months old. The baby was retarded, and this was more than the father could face. Sandra's mother worked long, hard hours for not much money, while Sandra not only worked part-time as soon as she could, but also had the main responsibility for her brother. Mother and daughter were united in seeing to it that Sandra would always be capable of earning a good living.

"I had to get good grades so I could get a scholarship to college," says Sandra, "and I had to be the best at whatever job I had. My brother is never going to be able to support himself, and I have to help him and my mother. She did so much for me I can never, ever make it up to her."

"That picnic?" Sandra says in response to John's query, "I have never been so angry in my life. Ingrid is a really impossible person. Theo was acting like a — a wimp. Felix is nice, I really like him, but he and Theo went off for a long walk, and left me to cope with Ingrid. And to top it all off, when I stalked off to the car and drank that whole flask of brandy, the last thing I saw before I passed out was Theo bending over me, saying, 'Do you really think you should have done that?' "

Everybody continued in therapy, and everybody

changed. Felix, instead of taking a second job to support Ingrid's extravagance, decided to go to graduate school. He arranged his working hours so that he could carry a full load of afternoon and evening classes, and he explained to Ingrid that she was simply going to have to economize. He explained it several times, and finally, after he returned a pair of hundred dollar shoes that she was sure she couldn't live without, she began listening.

Theo began to convince himself that making an occasional wrong decision was not likely to prove instantly fatal. He stopped being so critical of Sandra, and she, in turn, began encouraging him to relax and enjoy their time together as they had when they were first married.

Finally Ingrid decided that it was time for her to make an appointment with John.

John, at their first interview, realizes that Felix has not been exaggerating: Ingrid is an enchantingly pretty young woman. Ingrid is also clearly a young woman who is about to do her best to seduce her therapist.

"I came here prepared to dislike you, John," she purrs. "You've really messed up my life. Felix is so interested in the classes he's taking that he hardly has time to talk to me any more. Not that I care all *that* much, you understand; I've always believed in — well, let's call it open marriage, or free love. . . I can always find somebody who appreciates me. But anyway, I was starting to say that Felix never thought to tell me how good looking you are. I would really love to paint you. How about trading a few therapy sessions for a portrait? Not that I really need to get paid; you have such beautiful bone structure I'm just itching to get it down on canvas. Tell you what: I must be your last patient today, isn't that right? Why don't you come home with me and I'll fix you a couple of drinks and start sketching you? You can — um — you can see my etchings. Felix won't be home until about midnight."

John explains that he has a dinner date with his wife and their three children, and succeeds in getting the interview back on more conventional lines.

Ingrid is an only child, and came as a delightful surprise to her parents, who had been married for almost twenty years when she was born. One of her kindergarten teachers told her parents that she seemed to be exceptionally talented in the field of art, and her doting parents instantly arranged for private lessons. Ingrid really is talented, but she is also completely narcissistic; her art is the most important thing in the world to her, and she is convinced that it should also be the most important thing in the world to any right-minded person.

"Did you ever feel frustrated as a child?" asks John.

"No, never. Usually my parents would give me things as soon as I thought of wanting them, and if they did hold out once in awhile, I would just have a tantrum — that's when I was quite small of course. When I got older, I just wouldn't speak to them until they came through. Oh, John, I had such wonderful parents, I still miss them. They're both dead now. I married Felix because he said he would be not only a husband but a father to me — and he has been. A mother too. Until just lately. He's changed a lot, and I don't like it one bit."

Ingrid's impression of the picnic comes out like this: "Sandra was being a real bitch. Sometimes she acts as if she thinks she's my mother or something. If she were only half as nice a person as my mother, everything would be all right. So I forgot the lemonade, and I delayed lunch a little bit because I wanted to paint. So what? I don't see why she had to make such a big deal out of it."

Everybody continued in therapy for awhile longer. As Theo and Sandra stopped being judgmental of each other, they found that life could really be fun. They developed their rather underdeveloped senses of humor, and they stopped taking themselves and life in general so seriously. Felix charged ahead with his graduate studies, enjoying them more every day, and suddenly realized that he was no longer centering his life around Ingrid. He still loved her, he still admired her, he still wanted her — but she was no longer the pivot around which his whole world turned.

Ingrid reacted by having an affair with the instructor of her art class, but after discussing it with John, decided that she really didn't want to jeopardize her marriage. She needed Felix's love, and she came to realize that nobody else was likely to come close to giving her the almost unconditional approval that Felix did. So he was a little tight about money now, and preoccupied with his studies. Ingrid was quite confident that she could change all that, given a little time. And meanwhile, Felix was supportive of her one great passion: her art and her self.

Everybody is out of therapy now except Theo. John has suggested that he can stop pretty soon, but Theo still feels he needs more time, and John is willing to go along with him. It is the client who knows when therapy is finished.

In Felix's case, he terminated after about a year and a half, happily beginning his work toward a doctorate after finishing his master's degree. If he ever wants to consult John again, he will get a professional discount this time — he has earned it.

Ingrid stopped coming once she was thoroughly convinced that she could not seduce John. Ingrid has not changed a great deal; she never will. She has become a bit more tolerant of, and sensitive to, other people (especially Felix), but she is going to live out her life as the adored child of elderly parents, the talented artist who has a right to demand that the world conform to her wishes.

Sandra keeps seeing John for eleven months. Her progress is determined by Theo's progress: as he loosens up, so can she. At their last session, John suggests that she has now reached the point of diminishing returns: his fee is now $70.00 an hour, and he feels that from now on she simply won't get her money's worth. She can carry on now on her own.

Sandra leaps to her feet, hugs John, and says, "Do you really think so? You haven't heard what happened last night. I was helping Theo in the darkroom again (he seems to enjoy that nowadays) and I made the same darned mistake that I made a year ago, and ruined another batch of his pictures. But this time he laughed and said he could do them again."

"You know what you were doing, Sandra? Unconsciously, you were trying to test Theo, to see how he would react. That's why you made the mistake with the chemicals."

"You know what?" says Sandra happily, "I would like a cup of coffee!"

We hope this chapter has illustrated our belief that therapy is not just for those people who have some sort of serious mental illness. Therapy can be helpful for people who are just mildly neurotic, who feel that they are stuck in a bad place in their lives, who are reasonably happy but would like to increase their potential, whether it be in career advancement, creativity, or personal relations.

Three of our four characters entered therapy because they were unhappy for one reason or another. And when a married person goes into therapy, the marital relationship is going to change, and the spouse is going to have to accommodate the new relationship, with or without therapy. Ingrid is so self-centered that she is never going to be able to change much, but even she has come to face reality — bit by bit, perhaps, but closer than she has ever come before.

For most people, therapy will increase their sense of self-regard, will allow them to be more honest with themselves and to take more responsibility for their own lives. It will also make them more tolerant of others, help them to realize that what is important to them is not necessarily as important to others — and that that's all right. They can appreciate both themselves and other people better. They have, in a sense, come of age.

With or without therapy, we hope our readers will become active participants in getting their act together. Life, as we have mentioned now and then, is somewhat similar to a circus. Even in the best-prepared circus, the tightrope walker sometimes trips, the lion sometimes reacts differently, the tent sometimes springs a sudden leak. These things can be coped with if the performers are practiced and prepared. Similarly, some events in life are unpredictable; but if you have given some time to introspection, to examining your own life, to finding out what you really want and what you feel you owe to other people, you have a safety net of sorts. You are still going to have some surprises, and some of them are going to be unpleasant, but you will know who you are.

And knowing who you are is the first step toward

keeping your perspective, to balancing your needs with those of other people, to ending your life, when the time comes, feeling satisfied.

Or, to put it another way: to walking on air without stumbling.

Index

288

The Family That Plays
Together Stays Together

The Family That Plays Together Stays Together

(The Game "Gone Bananas")

This chapter is admittedly a "hard sell," and if you are one of those benighted souls who absolutely loathe all games more sedentary than racquetball, you might as well skip it.

If, however, you like board games either mildly or passionately, read on: we have a great one for you.

"Gone Bananas" is a microcosm of the psychic rewards and defeats that come to people in real life; the players, in order to "get all their buttons" (achieve a well-balanced personality) must get rewards for various facets of their personality: going to a party and avoiding social solecisms; playing the stock market and not suffering major business reverses; being graduated from college without being expelled — all this, while sidestepping not only the pitfalls of chance, but the aggressive tendencies of other players (one of the hazards of this game is getting "zapped" by your fellow players). These three paths to psychic success get you three of your four necessary buttons. The fourth comes after you have had a psychotherapy session. As in real life, this can be voluntary or involuntary; you can choose the psychotherapy route, or you can be committed to treatment, by landing in the wrong place at the wrong time.

You can collect "Wows" (feelings of achievement, good psychic feelings) by doing such things as completing your housekeeping in time for the late, late,

late show; cleaning out the fireplace and finding authentic Santa boots; or winning a tennis tournament using a croquet mallet. You can lose "Wows" by sitting in a dark closet and sulking all day or, while performing on your show, "What's Cooking?", burning the eggs on national television. And you not only lose "Wows" but collect "Ows" (guilt feelings) if you are so careless about brushing that you have to send your false teeth to the dentist to have a cavity filled, or if you forget the name of the President of the United States while you are introducing him to an ambassador. There are all sorts of possibilities. There are numerous ways of collecting "Wows" and getting rid of "Ows" (the board provides a handy park bench for the latter purpose).

You will find that some people play very aggressively (sometimes to their own eventual discomfiture) and others are inclined to take whatever Fate hands them. It takes some people all of thirty seconds to calculate the odds on rolling the dice one more time or being satisfied with their present winnings; other people never do learn. Playing this game tells you something about your own risk-taking or conservative nature, as well as other people's.

The game reflects the human condition in that it depends partly on chance — the roll of the dice. On the other hand, once you learn the odds, you have a great degree of control; that is, it is up to you to choose whether you want to bet all of your assets, or some of them, or none of them, on the next roll of the dice. You decide whether you take the high-risk, high-reward shortcuts, or the stodgier beaten path.

When John was beginning to develop this game, he felt that it might be useful in therapy to let clients discover whether they were inclined to take idiotic risks, whether they were too inclined to play it safe (and thereby lose everything) at all times, whether they were too aggressive or not assertive enough. As time went on, he began to believe that it might intrigue college students; still later, it seemed that it should appeal to most adults. The one group he hadn't counted on to embrace it with open arms was the juvenile set. Children as young as eight or nine (with a certain amount of adult guidance at first, of course) are highly enthusiastic about "Gone Bananas."

This, you will perceive, means that once your children are a bit beyond the preschool stage, "Gone Bananas" becomes a game for the whole family. The rules provide for several levels of play, so that you can tailor the difficulties to the abilities of your players. We really believe in the validity of the title of this chapter: "The family that plays together stays together." We don't suggest that you should limit your recreational activities entirely to evening after evening of "Gone Bananas." On the other hand, you could do worse!

Family communication nowadays tends to be limited. Everybody is busy, and television further short-circuits communication. This is truly a game with "a-peel," and as a happy by-product, it enhances communication among the players. You can laugh together. You can kid each other. You can think you are a certain winner, and at the last moment suddenly realize that your fourth grader has just managed to get her last button and is about to go out. And don't think that child isn't going to speak up about that in every social gathering for the next week.

The choices you make in playing "Gone Bananas" change depending on how the game is going and where the other players are — just like life. You try to take calculated risks, not absolutely wild ones — just like life. You win some and you lose some — just like life. It really does reflect the universal human condition.

Oh, yes, and it's fun to play.

You've been acting unbearably smug ever since they
used your picture in this book.

Now that you've found me, just let me finish this chapter — then I'll practice the act.

Dr. Lyke has since become boarded in the field of Clinical Psychology and has received a diploma signifying he is a Diplomate in Clinical Psychology, awarded by the American Board of Professional Psychology.

In recognition of excellent service to Metropolitan State College of Denver, he was awarded the title of Professor Emeritus, Department of Psychology, 1994.

He is also involved in completing a manuscript involving how we as a nation can capture the moral high ground of America's politics, published by iUniverse, Inc.

978-0-595-47421-9
0-595-47421-7

Printed in the United States
128311LV00003B/11/A

9 780595 474219